U·X·L
American Decades
1900·1909

Tom Pendergast
& Sara Pendergast,
Editors

U·X·L®

THOMSON
————————✦————————™
GALE

Detroit • New York • San Diego • San Francisco • Cleveland • New Haven, Conn. • Waterville, Maine • London • Munich

U•X•L American Decades, 1900–1909

Tom Pendergast and Sara Pendergast, Editors

Project Editors
Diane Sawinski, Julie L. Carnagie, and Christine Slovey

Editorial
Elizabeth Anderson

Permissions
Shalice Shah-Caldwell

Imaging and Multimedia
Dean Dauphinais

Product Design
Pamela A.E. Galbreath

Composition
Evi Seoud

Manufacturing
Rita Wimberley

For permission to use material from this product, submit your request via Web at http://www.gale-edit.com/permissions, or you may download our Permissions Request form and submit your request by fax or mail to:

Permissions Department
The Gale Group, Inc.
27500 Drake Rd.
Farmington Hills, MI 48331-3535
Permissions Hotline:
248-699-8006 or 800-877-4253, ext. 8006
Fax: 248-699-8074 or 800-762-4058

Cover photograph reproduced courtesy of the National Automobile Museum.

While every effort has been made to ensure the reliability of the information presented in this publication, The Gale Group, Inc. does not guarantee the accuracy of the data contained herein. The Gale Group, Inc. accepts no payment for listing; and inclusion in the publication of any organization, agency, institution, publication, service, or individual does not imply endorsement of the editors or publisher. Errors brought to the attention of the publisher and verified to the satisfaction of the publisher will be corrected in future editions.

Vol. 1: 0-7876-6455-3
Vol. 2: 0-7876-6456-1
Vol. 3: 0-7876-6457-X
Vol. 4: 0-7876-6458-8
Vol. 5: 0-7876-6459-6
Vol. 6: 0-7876-6460-X
Vol. 7: 0-7876-6461-8
Vol. 8: 0-7876-6462-6
Vol. 9: 0-7876-6463-4
Vol. 10: 0-7876-6464-2

LIBRARY OF CONGRESS CATALOGING-IN-PUBLICATION DATA

U•X•L American decades
   p. cm.
Includes bibliographical references and index.
   Contents: v. 1. 1900-1910—v. 2. 1910-1919—v. 3.1920-1929—v. 4. 1930-1939—v. 5. 1940-1949—v. 6. 1950-1959—v. 7. 1960-1969—v. 8. 1970-1979—v. 9.1980-1989—v. 10. 1990-1999.
   Summary: A ten-volume overview of the twentieth century which explores such topics as the arts, economy, education, government, politics, fashions, health, science, technology, and sports which characterize each decade.
   ISBN 0-7876-6454-5 (set: hardcover: alk. paper)
   1. United States—Civilization—20th century—Juvenile literature. 2. United States— History—20th century—Juvenile literature. [1. United States—Civilization—20th century. 2. United States—History—20th century.] I. UXL (Firm) II. Title: UXL American decades. III. Title: American decades.
E169.1.U88 2003
973.91—dc21
          2002010176

Printed in the United States of America
10 9 8 7 6 5 4 3 2 1

Contents

chapter four   *Government, Politics, and Law* . 57

Reader's Guide

U•X•L American Decades provides a broad overview of the major events and people that helped to shape American society throughout the twentieth century. Each volume in this ten-volume set chronicles a single decade and begins with an introduction to that decade and a timeline of major events in twentieth-century America. Following are eight chapters devoted to these categories of American endeavor:

• Arts and Entertainment

• Business and the Economy

• Education

• Government, Politics, and Law

• Lifestyles and Social Trends

• Medicine and Health

• Science and Technology

• Sports

These chapters are then divided into five sections:

Chronology: A timeline of significant events within the chapter's particular field.

Overview: A summary of the events and people detailed in that chapter.

Headline Makers: Short biographical accounts of key people and their achievements during the decade.

❖ **Topics in the News:** A series of short topical essays describing events and people within the chapter's theme.

✤ **For More Information:** A section that lists books and Web sites directing the student to further information about the events and people covered in the chapter.

OTHER FEATURES

Each volume of *U•X•L American Decades* contains more than eighty black-and-white photographs and illustrations that bring the events and people discussed to life and sidebar boxes that expand on items of high interest to readers. Concluding each volume is a general bibliography of books and Web sites that explore the particular decade in general and a thorough subject index that allows readers to easily locate the events, people, and places discussed throughout that volume of *U•X•L American Decades*.

COMMENTS AND SUGGESTIONS

We welcome your comments on *U•X•L American Decades* and suggestions for other history topics to consider. Please write: Editors, *U•X•L American Decades*, U•X•L, 27500 Drake Rd., Farmington Hills, MI 48331-3535; call toll-free: 1-800-877-4253; fax: 248-699-8097; or send e-mail via http://www.galegroup.com.

Chronology of the 1900s

1900: Thomas Alva Edison invents the nickel-based alkaline storage battery.

1900: German scientists invent the modern pendulum seismograph to detect earthquakes.

1900: Sigmund Freud's *On the Interpretation of Dreams* is published.

1900: The U.S. Army's Yellow Fever Commission identifies the mosquito as the carrier of the deadly disease.

1900: **January 29** In professional baseball, Byron Bancroft "Ban" Johnson forms the American League by expanding the former minor-league Western Association to include eastern cities.

1900: **March 14** Congress passes the Gold Standard Act to improve the national economy. The Act establishes that all U.S. currency is backed by and exchangeable for gold.

1900: **March 31** The first national advertisement for automobiles appears in *The Saturday Evening Post.*

1900: **May** The Russians occupy Manchuria, and their forces massacre an estimated forty-five thousand Chinese inhabitants.

1900: **July 2** The first Zeppelin dirigible is flown in Germany.

1900: **September 17** The newly formed United Mine Workers (UMW) union stages its first strike in Pennsylvania with nearly one hundred thousand miners participating.

1900: December 14 Max Planck, a German physicist, announces the basis of quantum theory: light rays are emitted in discrete amounts called quanta.

1901: The Mercedes motorcar is introduced by German auto maker Gottlieb Daimler.

1901: The Trans-Siberian railway is completed between Moscow and Port Arthur.

1901: January 22 Britain's Queen Victoria dies. Her son, Edward VII, succeeds her to the throne.

1901: January 27 Italian opera composer Giuseppe Verdi dies.

1901: February 25 Formed by a merger of ten companies, U.S. Steel is established as the world's largest industrial corporation.

1901: March 13 Andrew Carnegie, the steel tycoon, donates $2.2 million to fund a New York public library system.

1901: June The College Board's entrance examination is given to high school students for the first time.

1901: June 24 Painter Pablo Picasso opens his first exhibition at Galeries Vollard, Paris.

1901: September The Socialist Revolutionary Party of Russia is founded.

1901: September 6 President William McKinley is assassinated by Leon Czolgosz in Buffalo, New York. Theodore Roosevelt becomes the twenty-sixth president of the United States.

1901: September 7 The Boxer Rebellion in China ends with the signing of the Peace of Peking between China and major European nations.

1901: December 10 Sweden awards the first Nobel Prizes for achievement in the fields of physics, chemistry, medicine, literature, and peace.

1901: December 12 Guglielmo Marconi receives the first transatlantic wireless message in Newfoundland.

1902: Ivan Pavlov, a Russian physiologist and psychologist, discovers conditioned reflexes.

1902: January 1 At the first Tournament of Roses Association football game, held in Pasadena, California, the University of Michigan defeats Stanford University by a score of 49-0. The Rose Bowl becomes an annual event in 1916.

1902: **May 31** The Peace of Vereeniging ends the Boer War in South Africa.

1902: **June 1** The state of Maryland passes the nation's first worker's compensation law to protect workers injured on the job.

1902: **October 1–13** In baseball's first World Series, Boston defeats Pittsburgh five games to three.

1902: **December 21** Guglielmo Marconi transmits the first wireless signals across the Atlantic Ocean.

1903: Norwegian explorer Roald Amundsen begins the first successful voyage through the Northwest Passage, the narrow sea connecting the Atlantic and Pacific Oceans.

1903: **February** The *Ladies' Home Journal* becomes the first American magazine to reach one million paid subscriptions.

1903: **April 27** The Supreme Court upholds a clause in the Alabama constitution that effectively prohibits African Americans from voting.

1903: **May 23** Wisconsin becomes the first state to hold direct primary elections.

1903: **December 17** In Kitty Hawk, North Carolina, Wilbur and Orville Wright make their first sustained flight, setting the stage for the development of the airline industry.

1904: French sculptor Auguste Rodin creates one of his best-known works, *The Thinker.*

1904: The Rolls-Royce automobile company is established in Britain.

1904: Italian Giacomo Puccini composes his opera *Madame Butterfly.*

1904: **February 8–9** The Russo-Japanese War begins when the Japanese launch an attack on the Russian fleet.

1904: **March 23** The first color newspaper photograph is published in the *London Daily Illustrated Mirror.*

1904: **April 22** The Panama Canal officially comes under the control of the U.S. government.

1904: **April 30** The St. Louis World's Fair opens.

1904: **May 5** Denton "Cy" Young pitches the first perfect game under modern baseball rules: not allowing any opposing player to reach first base.

1904: **September 1** Helen Keller, who lost both her sight and hearing at age two, graduates from Radcliffe College.

1904: **October 27** The New York City subway opens, becoming the country's first rapid transit system.

1904: **November 8** Theodore Roosevelt is elected president of the United States. Republican majorities in both houses of Congress are increased.

1905: Doctor Ludvig Hecktoen proves humans can transmit measles to one another.

1905: American May Sutton becomes the first non-Briton to win the Wimbledon tennis championship, held at the All-England Club.

1905: **January 22** The "Bloody Sunday" massacre in Saint Petersburg sparks the Russian Revolution.

1905: **May 5** The *Chicago Defender,* the first major black newspaper, begins publication.

1905: **June 27** The Industrial Workers of the World (IWW) is organized by a combination of miners, socialists, and anarchists who are dedicated to overthrowing the capitalist system.

1905: **June 30** Albert Einstein announces his special theory of relativity. On September 27, he issues a second paper on the subject containing his famous formulation $E=mc^2$.

1905: **July 9** The "Niagara Movement" is established at Niagara Falls, Canada, where a group of black leaders (including W. E. B. Du Bois) advocate full civil and political rights for African Americans.

1905: **September 1** Alberta and Saskatchewan are made provinces of Canada.

1905: **September 27** Norway gains its independence from Sweden.

1906: The Meat Inspection Act is passed by Congress after widespread public concern over unsanitary conditions in the meat-packing industry.

1906: **February** Upton Sinclair publishes *The Jungle,* a novel depicting the horrible conditions in the meat-packing industry. The work prompts the passage of the Meat Inspection Act and influences the Pure Food and Drug Act.

1906: **March 7** Finland becomes the first nation to grant women's suffrage.

1906: **April 6** Mount Vesuvius erupts, destroying several towns near Naples, Italy.

1906: April 18 San Francisco sustains a major earthquake and subsequent fire, which destroy much of the city. The devastation leaves 250,000 people homeless. 25,000 buildings destroyed, and 500 dead.

1906: April 19 French chemist Pierre Curie dies.

1906: October 22 French Impressionist master Paul Cézanne dies.

1906: November Leon Trotsky, one of the leaders of the 1905 Russian Revolution, is exiled to Siberia.

1906: December 31 Lee De Forest invents the triode vacuum tube, which made possible the transmission of human voice, music, and other broadcast signals via wireless telephony.

1907: The first helicopter flight takes place in France.

1907: Maria Montessori opens her first school for average children in Rome.

1907: March 12 Alain Locke becomes the first African American to receive a Rhodes Scholarship. No other African American scholar will be so honored for half a century.

1907: July 8 Florenz Ziegfeld's musical revue, the *Ziegfeld Follies,* opens in New York.

1907: August 24 The works of American impressionist painter Mary Cassatt are displayed in New York.

1907: September 12 The *Lusitania,* the world's largest steamship, completes its first voyage.

1907: December 3 Actress Mary Pickford makes her stage debut in *The Warrens of Virginia.*

1907: December 16 The "Great White Fleet," a flotilla of sixteen U.S. warships, embarks on a cruise around the world to demonstrate American naval power.

1908: The first Geiger counter is developed by German physicist Hans Geiger and British physicist Ernest Rutherford.

1908: The first skyscraper, which stands forty-seven stories (612 feet) tall, is completed in New York City.

1908: May Mother's Day is observed for the first time in Philadelphia, Pennsylvania.

1908: May 26 Petroleum production begins in the Middle East.

....

1908: October 1 The Ford Motor Company unveils the Model T automobile. The $825 price tag makes it possible for people with moderate incomes to purchase an automobile.

1908: October 5 Bulgaria declares its independence from the Ottoman Empire.

1908: October 6 Austria annexes the former Turkish provinces of Bosnia and Herzegovina, setting the stage for events that will spark World War I six years later.

1908: November 3 Republican William Howard Taft is elected the twenty-seventh president of the United States.

1908: November 9 The U.S. Supreme Court upholds a Kentucky law prohibiting racial integration in private schools in *Berea College* v. *Kentucky.*

1908: December 26 Jack Johnson becomes the first black world heavyweight boxing champion.

1909: February 12 The National Association for the Advancement of Colored People (NAACP) is founded in New York City.

1909: March 23 Former President Theodore Roosevelt leaves for a safari in Africa. He is paid $50,000 to publish his account of the trip.

1909: April 6 U.S. Navy commander Robert Peary reaches the North Pole.

1909: May 3 The first wireless press message is sent from New York to Chicago.

1909: July 12 The Sixteenth Amendment to the Constitution, authorizing income taxes, is ratified by Congress.

1909: August 2 The Indian-head penny, which had been in circulation for fifty years, is replaced by the Lincoln penny.

The 1900s: An Overview

During the first decade of the twentieth century the United States was at a unique moment in its history. America was poised to take the lead in international politics, economics, and culture. The 1900s was a decade when many Americans embraced the new and modern: the automobile was becoming a common sight on the nation's roadways; the airplane was being perfected; modern styles of art, music, dance, and architecture were being introduced; scientific advances were announced in biology, psychology, and in the physical sciences; and reformers labored to alter American politics and society.

In 1900, Great Britain's Queen Victoria reigned over the largest empire in history. Her rule extended over possessions on every continent that comprised 11 million square miles and 400 million people. By the dawn of the year 2000, the British Empire would be largely dismantled and the United States would be recognized as the world's lone superpower. This transformation was accomplished by the modernist spirit that pervaded America throughout the twentieth century, especially during the 1900s. It was in this decade that the United States emerged as an industrial giant and was soon outproducing Britain in coal, steel, and iron. This new economic strength resulted in the nation's movement away from the isolationism, the lack of involvement in European affairs, that characterized it in the nineteenth century.

Led by its vigorous and dynamic president, Theodore Roosevelt, the United States began to actively engage with territories located in the Caribbean Sea and the Pacific Ocean, including Latin America, the Philippines, and China. International relations was not the only dramatic change to occur in American politics. The era also saw the rise of the progressive movement, in which many members of the urban middle-class began to work for legislative (governmental) reform. Some progressives were most concerned with ridding the cities of vice and corruption as they demanded the prohibition of alcohol, closed brothels, and targeted crooked politicians. Other progressives attacked corporate trusts that limited competition in the marketplace. The 1900s saw great achievements in regulating unlawful business practices, conserving natural resources, opening up the electoral (voting) process, and improving working conditions for women and children.

Still, reformers were not successful in all areas. The condition of African Americans was a source of great concern. Blacks had few political and civil rights throughout much of the country and they were largely segregated from white society. The races were separated in terms of public facilities, transportation, and housing in the 1900s. Violence against blacks was rampant: there were more than one hundred lynchings in 1900 alone. It would not be until the 1960s that African Americans gained their full civil rights.

While the tone of much of the 1900s was modernist and progressive, a significant portion of the population was unnerved at the rapid transformation of society. Many Americans expressed nostalgia for the traditions, manners, and customs of the nineteenth century. They were uneasy with the expanding roles played by women, immigrants, and minorities across the land. Among the most vocal of this group were the millions of religious fundamentalists who opposed advances in the empirical sciences. Business leaders became distressed with the rise of industrial labor unions that demanded better treatment and pay for their workers. Many rural citizens were distressed with the increased power of the nation's urban centers, which were teeming with immigrants from all over the world. They claimed these new citizens were dirty, uneducated, and not sufficiently loyal to the United States. Programs were introduced nationwide that proclaimed the necessity of "Americanizing" these immigrants in the ways and customs of American life.

On April 10, 1899, a young Theodore Roosevelt called on his fellow Americans to meet the challenges of the dawning age. "The twentieth century looms before us big with the fate of many nations," he said. "If we stand idly by, if we seek merely swollen, slothful ease and ignoble peace, if we shrink from the hard contests where men must win at hazard of their lives and at the risk of all they hold dear, then the bolder and stronger peoples will pass us by, and will win for themselves the domination of the world."

While many of Roosevelt's contemporaries worried less about the struggle for world power than about the struggle for daily survival, they were sharply aware of the United States's place on the world stage, even if they were uncertain or divided about the role the nation would eventually play.

chapter one *Arts and Entertainment*

1900: **February 5** The drama *Sappho* by Clyde Fitch premieres in New York, but is closed by the police after only twenty-nine performances due to complaints of "immorality."

1900: **April 23** Buffalo Bill Cody's *Wild West Show* opens at Madison Square Garden.

1900: **April 30** Railroad engineer Casey Jones dies as he jams the brakes on his wreck-bound train, saving all his passengers. Jones soon is immortalized as an American hero when Wallace Saunders composes a popular song about him.

1901: **February 2** The opera *Tosca* by Giacomo Puccini debuts in New York.

1901: **February 21** Vaudeville performers organize to strike and protest against the inclusion of motion pictures on vaudeville bills.

1901: **March 13** Andrew Carnegie, the steel tycoon, donates $2.2 million to fund a New York public library system.

1901: **June 24** Painter Pablo Picasso opens his first exhibition at Galeries Vollard, Paris.

1901: **December 10** Sweden awards the first Nobel Prizes for achievement in the fields of physics, chemistry, medicine, literature, and peace.

1902: **April 16** Tally's Electric Theater, the first theater solely devoted to presenting motion pictures, opens in Los Angeles.

1902: **May 1** Georges Méliès premieres *A Trip to the Moon,* which is considered to be the first science fiction film.

1902: **December 21** Guglielmo Marconi transmits the first wireless signals across the Atlantic Ocean.

1903: **February** The *Ladies' Home Journal* becomes the first American magazine to reach one million paid subscriptions.

1903: **May 6** Emma Lazarus's poem "The New Colossus" (1883) is affixed to the Statue of Liberty.

1903: **September 12** African American composer Scott Joplin's ragtime opera, *A Guest of Honor,* begins a Midwest tour.

1904: **January 17** Russian writer Anton Chekhov's play *The Cherry Orchard* premieres in Moscow.

1904: **March 23** The first color newspaper photograph is published in the *London Daily Illustrated Mirror.*

1904: **April 30** The St. Louis World's Fair opens.

1904: **September 1** Helen Keller, who lost both her sight and hearing at age two, graduates from Radcliffe College.

1905: **May 5** The *Chicago Defender,* the first major black newspaper, begins publication.

1905: June The era of the nickelodeon begins when Harry Davis's Pittsburgh movie theater offers continuous movie showings. By the end of the decade more than eight thousand nickel-admission movie theaters are in operation.

1906: January 8 Protestors in New York City claim *The Clansman,* a play based upon Thomas Dixon's novel, is racist.

1906: February Upton Sinclair publishes *The Jungle,* a novel depicting the horrible conditions in the meat-packing industry. The work prompts the passage of the Meat Inspection Act and influences the Pure Food and Drug Act.

1906: April 14 President Theodore Roosevelt coins the term "muckraking" when he criticizes journalists who expose corruption and abuses and miss the larger picture.

1906: April 18 A major earthquake and fire destroy much of San Francisco.

1907: June 10 French motion picture pioneers Auguste and Louis Lumière announce they have developed a method of producing color film.

1907: July 8 Florenz Ziegfeld's musical revue, the *Ziegfeld Follies,* opens in New York.

1907: August 24 The works of American impressionist painter Mary Cassatt are displayed in New York.

1907: December 3 Actress Mary Pickford makes her stage debut in *The Warrens of Virginia.*

1908: February 11 Thomas Edison and his film-producing partners win a series of patent infringement lawsuits that keeps their competitors out of the film business. Edison claimed his competition illegally infringed on his patented motion picture camera technology.

1908: March The Original Independent Show, organized in New York, includes works by American painters Edward Hopper, George Bellows, and Rockwell Kent.

1908: September 6 Israel Zangwill's play *The Melting Pot* opens in New York City. The title becomes an internationally recognized description of the United States.

1909: March 23 Former President Theodore Roosevelt leaves for a safari in Africa. He is paid fifty million dollars to publish his account of the trip.

1909: May 1 American painter John Singer Sargent's works are hailed at the Royal Academy Art Show in London.

1909: May 3 The first wireless press message is sent from New York to Chicago.

※ *Overview* . . . .

At the dawn of the twentieth century, many Americans were filled with both pride in their nation's past achievements and confidence in their bright future. Technological and manufacturing advances since the Civil War (1861–65) had allowed the United States to become an international power, and its citizens enjoyed the highest standard of living in the world. Most Americans believed that the new century would look much like the old century: Moral values would remain constant, scientific progress would continue to benefit society, and traditional themes in arts and culture would endure. When we look back, however, we can see problems that might have tempered the confidence and optimism that characterized the public's mood.

In the arts, a cultural gap between the classes was becoming increasingly evident. The lower classes, which often earned less than five dollars per week, saw the arts as a luxury they could not afford. Those at the bottom of the economic pyramid generally filled their free time at penny arcades, the nickelodeon, and dance halls, or in activities related to their ethnic traditions. In contrast, the cultural elite continued to celebrate "highbrow" arts such as the opera, the symphony, Broadway theater, and the pastime of collecting Asian and European antiquities. The middle class patronized the museums and libraries built by the elite's philanthropy. They also enjoyed family-friendly vaudeville shows. At home, middle-class entertainment centered on the piano or phonograph in the parlor.

"Popular culture" was an unknown term in this era without television or radio, but it was fast becoming a phenomenon. Mass marketing was succeeding at bringing mainstream entertainment to a large portion of the population. However, the cultural elite remained immersed in the "genteel tradition" that emphasized the romantic idealism and studied refinement of the past. The nineteenth century and its grandeur in painting, art, music, and literature was viewed as the height of human artistic achievement. Those artists, writers, and musicians who dared to be experimental and creative were met with rejection and ridicule. Americans in the first decade of the twentieth century were content with traditional styles in the arts. American art and literature had advanced dramatically in the 1800s and was finally up to European standards. The so-called custodians of culture were satisfied with these accomplishments and did not seek change.

Still, some individual artists and writers were innovators who began to challenge popular norms and tastes. Individually, and in groups or "movements," they pushed the American arts toward a dynamic path that would characterize much of the twentieth century. The term "modernists" has been used to describe those cultural innovators who deliberately set out to diverge from established traditions in the arts.

While most Americans had not embraced modernism, the years 1900 to 1909 were not without some innovations and accomplishments. In literature, Theodore Dreiser's *Sister Carrie* (1900) shocked readers with its frank treatment of sexuality. Although the novel was praised for its gritty realism, its publishers suppressed the work for years for fear that it would disturb readers. Some writers like Gertrude Stein left the United States for the more liberal Europe in hopes of finding an audience. On the art scene, critics were appalled by the "modern art" that was emerging. The slum life depicted in "Ash Can"-style paintings scandalized those who objected to its unsavory subject matter and loose painterly style. In the field of architecture, Frank Lloyd Wright was building his long, low, environmentally friendly Prairie Style designs while architects from the Chicago school were creating gigantic steel skyscrapers. The rising Arts and Crafts design movement announced a transition away from the elaborate and ornate style that characterized the Victorian era. Even music was a center of innovation, as Scott Joplin developed ragtime and Ma Rainey sang the blues. Despite these and other cultural innovators' best efforts, however, the mainstream public remained largely unresponsive to their creations.

No means of mass communication yet existed that could offer the entire nation common information and ideas. Print was the first medium to reach a national audience, but it was stratified. The elite read literary journals such as *The Atlantic* and *Harper's Bazaar,* which filled their pages with works by respected authors like Mark Twain, William Dean Howells, and Sarah Orne Jewett. On the other hand, the masses read serialized romances and adventure stories printed on inexpensive paper. Among the works most popular with the mainstream public were Thomas Dixon's *The Clansman* (1905), a racist view of the Old South; Owen Wister's *The Virginian* (1902), a novel of Western heroism; and Alice Hegan Rice's *Mrs. Wiggs of the Cabbage Patch* (1901). Jack London became wealthy with the success of his many adventure novels like *The Call of the Wild* (1903) and *White Fang* (1906). Horatio Alger was another prominent writer whose 135 rags-to-riches tales found mass acceptance.

Theodore Dreiser (1871–1945) Born into a large family troubled by poverty, writer Theodore Dreiser was shaped by his bleak childhood to adopt a naturalistic view of the world. Dreiser considered humans to be creatures plagued by blind forces and their own passions in an amoral, uncaring universe. He translated this attitude into realistic fiction with his first novel *Sister Carrie* (1900), which many considered scandalous and unfit for the reading public. For much of his career Dreiser faced censorship, condemnation, and controversy. Dreiser's most impressive novels include *The Titan* (1914), *The "Genius"* (1915), and *An American Tragedy* (1925), which is considered to be his masterpiece. *Photograph courtesy of the Library of Congress.*

Isadora Duncan (1878–1927) Isadora Duncan revolutionized American modern dance with her spontaneous movements and open sensuality. Duncan's dance came to symbolize liberation from the stagnant traditions of European culture. While she was praised for her innovation, many Americans considered her suggestive style obscene. Duncan spent much of her life in Europe and the Soviet Union as an expatriate (one who lives somewhere other than one's native country). Duncan became involved in radical politics and saw her liberated dance moves as mirroring the revolutionaries' liberation from outmoded political systems. *Photograph reproduced by permission of AP/Wide World Photos.*

Robert Henri (1865–1929) Painter Robert Henri led a revolt in American modern art circles when he and a group of like-minded artists, referred to as "The Eight," complained that American art should be free from European domination. Henri believed that art should be accessible to all Americans, not only to the experts. One of his most lasting contributions was to advocate the idea that urban landscapes were a subject worthy of serious art. While many complained that Henri's work had an element of coarseness, others viewed it as a counterpart to the social realism movement in American literature. At his death, Henri was hailed as a great influence on modern American art. *Photograph reproduced by permission of Dover Publications, Inc.*

Scott Joplin (1868–1917) Scott Joplin was the foremost pianist and composer of ragtime, which was a lively and danceable form of music known for its "ragged" rhythm. The son of a former slave, Joplin was drawn to the African American musical style and produced some of its greatest compositions. His "Maple Leaf Rag" (1899) is one of the most famous American tunes. Ragtime allowed for a certain amount of improvisation and served as an important foundation for the evolving art of jazz music. Joplin wanted to be recognized not just as a popular songwriter but also as a composer of artistic merit. He was widely hailed for the ragtime opera *Treemonisha* (1911).

Jack London (1876–1916) Born into poverty, writer Jack London left school at age fourteen in search of a life of adventure. He displayed an early love for the sea and worked as both an oyster pirate and a member of the California Fish Patrol. London eventually became a writer and based many of his stories on his adventures and nature. He introduced a masculinized style to American fiction, emphasizing a fascination with strength, violence, and the primitive. His most popular works include *White Fang* (1906) and *Call of the Wild* (1903). *Photograph courtesy of the Library of Congress.*

Edwin Stanton Porter (1869–1941) Director and filmmaker Edwin Porter was one of the most important technical innovators in early American cinema. In 1898, Porter's work resulted in steadier and brighter film projection. As an employee of Thomas Edison, Porter was placed in charge of all the Edison Company's film projects. He expanded the boundaries of cinema by experimenting with split screens, double exposures, and special effects. In 1903, Porter produced several landmark films. *The Life of a Fireman* (1903) was one of the first films to have a plot that extended beyond one scene and the first to be edited in the cutting room. Porter's *The Great Train Robbery* (1903) is considered to be America's first Western movie.

Edith Wharton (1862–1937) Born into a distinguished family, novelist Edith Wharton was raised in New York's high society. Her writings often chronicled the individual's conflict with the constraints of social convention. Her two most famous novels, *Ethan Frome* (1911) and *The Age of Innocence* (1920), examined the lives of individuals who are crushed by conformist attitudes. In 1920, she was awarded the Pulitzer Prize for the latter work. Wharton spent much of her adulthood as a journalist in Europe. By the time of her death she was consistently named one of the "greatest women in America." *Photograph reproduced by permission of Pictorial Parade, Inc.*

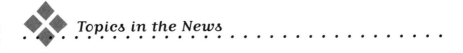

❖ AMERICAN IMPRESSIONISM AND REALISM

American artists were strongly influenced by the style known as French Impressionism, which reduced solid objects to broad smudges and murky shadows in order to emphasize emotion over precision. This style was praised for its mysterious and romantic quality. Mary Cassatt (1844–1936) is considered the first "pure" Impressionist born in America. She and several other leading American Impressionists were dissatisfied with the conservatism of the art scene and its huge exhibitions that confused viewers with a jumble of various styles. They organized themselves as "The Ten" and agreed to annually and exclusively exhibit their works together. Their goal was to promote American Impressionism to collectors. The style soon spread throughout the nation as regional Impressionists appeared in Boston, Pennsylvania, Indiana, and San Francisco.

Other artists were inspired by these Impressionists and began to assert the notion that American art should be free from European influences and artificial standards. They challenged Eurocentric (favoring Europe) tastes by adopting the style of Realism, which emphasized realistic subject matter and offered uncompromising depictions of urban life.

❖ REALISM DOMINATES THE LITERARY SCENE

At the beginning of the 1900s, much of American literature imitated European literary forms with their refined styles that celebrated romantic rather than realistic experience. William Dean Howells (1837–1920), a novelist, playwright, and critic, is called the "father of American Realism" because he demanded that his work reflect everyday reality. He argued that realistic detail was necessary for strong writing. His characters spoke in the language of the common man, lived ordinary lives, and were psychologically complex. Other writers such as Frank Norris, Stephen Crane, Hamlin Garland, and Theodore Dreiser were even more uncompromising in their depiction of reality. They subscribed to the Naturalistic theory, which held that a writer should adopt an objective view toward the chosen material. Dreiser's *Sister Carrie* (1900), considered the century's best example of a naturalistic novel, is an unflinching portrait of a young girl's life of poverty, loneliness, and immorality.

Although several important female and minority authors such as Sarah Orne Jewett (1849–1909) Waddell Chesnutt (1853–1932), wrote books during the decade, most publishers did not choose to offer works

Year	Writer
1901	René F. A. Sully-Prudhomme, France
1902	Theodor Mommensen, Germany
1903	Bjornsterne Brornson, Norway
1904	Frédéric Mistral, France
1904	Jose Echegaray, Spain
1905	Henryk Sienkewicz, Poland
1906	Giosué Carducci, Italy
1907	Rudyard Kipling, Great Britain
1908	Rudolph Eueken, Germany
1909	Selma Lagerlof, Sweden

whose subject matter would not appeal to a wide readership. Many of these authors achieved the most success by serializing their work (writing weekly or monthly installments printed in national magazines).

The Western was an especially popular genre of literature during this period. Owen Wister (1860–1938) and Zane Grey (1875–1939) became best-selling authors with their novels about cowboy heroes on the vanishing frontier. Native Americans also wrote about their experiences in the West. Among the most prominent was Charles Alexander Eastman (1858–1939), the son of a Sioux father and a white mother, who straddled both cultures and was conflicted in his loyalties. In 1902, he wrote, "The Indian no longer exists as a free man. Those remnants that dwell upon the reservations present only a sort of a tableau, a fictional copy of the past."

❖ THE RISE OF THE MOTION PICTURE INDUSTRY

The film industry was in its infancy during the first decade of the twentieth century. The earliest films were crudely produced short features presented at penny arcades on kinescopes, hand-turned viewing machines that presented about thirty seconds of action. In 1902, Thomas Tally's Electric Theater in Los Angeles opened its doors, featuring continuous films from 7:30 P.M. to 10:30 P.M. and changing its program every month. It

Film Pioneers

The early American film industry was centered not in Hollywood but on the East Coast. Several production companies, including Edison, Biograph, Vitagraph, Essanay, and Lublin, competed vigorously. By 1907, the industry had developed standard practices and a three-part structure: production, distribution, and exhibition. The following year the leading companies combined to form the Motion Picture Patents Company, a monopolistic trust that controlled all aspects of the industry. The earliest silent films contained simplistic plots and broad pantomime acting in which actors overemphasized their emotions with dramatic gestures. Still, the industry thrived as audiences filled storefront theaters and nickelodeons to gaze upon the cinema screen.

was the first permanent movie theater in the United States. The Electric Theater and other "storefront" movie houses had minimal overhead expenses, as they did not book live acts or musical groups, but they were still financially risky operations.

In 1905, a Pittsburgh storefront theater opened with plush seats, a piano, frequent program changes, and a nickel admission. Audiences flocked to this "nickelodeon," and within four years there were more than four thousand nickelodeons in the country. By 1908, an estimated eighty million nickelodeon tickets were sold every week in America.

Early cinema was less concerned with a film's artistic merit than its financial success. Movie producers made dozens of inexpensive comedies and melodramas dealing with limited subjects. Although a few films attempted to be creative and challenging to a mass audience, the bigger American studios failed to produce longer films on more serious subjects. It was believed a film audience would not sit through a single picture that was longer than fifteen minutes.

Silent cinema had a number of problems: static, lifeless scenes; overly simplistic plots; outdoor shots that were frequently ruined by foul weather; and inexperienced performers. Respectable stage performers and vaudeville headliners refused to be seen on screen. Actors who did appear in movies received little acclaim and were paid an average of only five dollars a day. The studios sold the earliest films as "brand" name entertain-

The Great Train Robbery

Director Edwin Porter's *The Great Train Robbery* (1903) is a true landmark in cinema history. Filmed in rural New Jersey and starring Bronco Billy Anderson, it established many of the essential characters, plots, and situations of the Western film genre. Within its ten-minute running time it included a train robbery, a saloon fight, gunplay, and a pursuit on horseback. These conventions were repeated in hundreds of Westerns throughout the century. The film is also noted for its technical achievements. It was one of the longest films of its era and depicted a complicated story line. Porter enhanced his film with such new technological camera tricks as the pan and close-up. He also increased the suspense through skillful editing. *The Great Train Robbery* was the first indication that film could become a legitimate art form.

ment in the first years of the century, prohibiting actors' and directors' names from appearing on screen. Production companies feared that interest in the players would detract from interest in the whole product. The star system did not enter the movie industry until the 1910s. Mary Pickford (1893–1979), who later became an international movie star, was originally known only as "The Biograph Comedy Girl." Early in the 1910s film producers recognized the profits and large audiences that stars would attract and soon granted them much publicity.

While the upper, middle, and working classes all enjoyed films, some Americans claimed the cinema fostered immorality. They complained that unattended children made up a large portion of the audience, as their working-class parents viewed the cinema as a source of cheap childcare. Critics also stated that the darkened theaters were filled with "foreigners," "sailors," and illicit sexual activity. Finally, complaints surrounded the content of the films themselves. Critics said movies displayed vulgar themes, low humor, and titillating scenes. By 1909, the movie industry had created a National Board of Censorship to improve film content, and reformers continued to advocate improved movie house conditions. Despite all these problems, the cinema industry thrived and was aided by creative individuals who nurtured it until it achieved artistic excellence in the following decade.

One of the most influential artists of the decade was photographer Alfred Stieglitz (1864–1946). He revolutionized the art world through his attempts to prove that photography was equal to painting as an art form. During the 1890s Stieglitz was a leader of the "pictorial" photography movement, which, like Impressionism, emphasized composition and suggestion over detail. In 1902, he and several fellow photographers formed the Photo-Secession, a group of artists dedicated to advancing pictorial photography. Within a decade the Photo-Secessionists had convinced the artistic establishment that photography was a valid fine art form.

❖ THE TRUE AMERICAN ART FORM: MUSIC

The art form that had evolved the most into its own American style by the turn of the century was popular music. A medley of prominent musical forms during the era included jazz, ballads, show tunes, the blues, and ragtime. Music could be heard in all corners of society, from the modest dwellings of immigrants who sang of their homelands to the grand mansions of the cultural elite who patronized the opera and the symphonies. The most important factor affecting music during the 1900s was the rapid expansion of the "music industry," which produced sheet music, instruments, phonographs, and record cylinders intended to promote and play popular songs.

American music during the first decade of the twentieth century was marked by its great diversity. By 1900, the center of the music industry had moved to New York City. Aspiring musicians and composers played their latest tunes for potential performers and agencies in hopes of creating a hit song. Minstrel shows, which presented stereotypically racist displays of African American life, remained popular throughout much of the nation. Still, some black performers such as Bob Cole (1868–1911), James Weldon Johnson (1871–1938), and J. Rosamund Johnson (1873–1954) were able to break free from the minstrel traditions to produce sophisticated vaudeville shows and Broadway musicals. In 1900, the Johnsons composed "Lift Every Voice and Sing," considered by many to be the African American anthem.

African Americans also played pivotal roles in the development of the blues, jazz, and ragtime, all musical forms that were born in America. Rag-

OPPOSITE PAGE
The Steerage (1907), by Alfred Stieglitz.
Reproduced by permission of the Art Institute of Chicago.

time was the most popular piano rhythm in the 1900s. Its "ragged" syncopated beat captured the public's imagination. Scott Joplin (1868–1917) was a popular composer and became the "Ragtime King."

Both jazz and blues music evolved during the 1900s, largely due to the efforts of African Americans. Although the term "jazz" would not be coined for more than a decade, the improvisational instrumental form probably originated from the parade and funeral music played in New Orleans, Louisiana. Among the most noteworthy players and composers of early 1900s "jazz" were Joe "King" Oliver (1885–1938), a trumpeter and cornet player, and Ferdinand "Jelly Roll" Morton (1885–1942), a pianist. Although many whites scorned jazz, it emerged by the 1920s as a significant African American contribution to American music.

Like jazz, the blues originated from the African American experience following the Civil War. An outgrowth of Mississippi Delta field songs, with their calls and responses, the blues expressed loneliness, woe, humor, and defiance. Although W.C. Handy (1873–1958) published the first blues songs, most historians consider Ma Rainey the bearer of the blues to America through her minstrel performances. Born Gertrude Pridgett (1886–1930), Rainey sang poignant songs that won her acclaim and the title "mother of the blues."

Each of the era's musical forms was distributed across the country primarily through sheet music and player piano rolls. When, in 1902, opera singer Enrico Caruso (1873–1921) recorded ten arias for the Gramophone and Typewriter Company to much acclaim and great sales, the American music industry realized the commercial possibilities of recorded music. Soon nearly every major operatic and popular musical performer was making recordings, and the record industry quickly expanded. By the early 1900s, the record and record player became not a novelty but a necessity, both to those who produced American music and those who wanted to hear it.

*Composer Scott Joplin,
the king of ragtime.
Reproduced by permission of
Fisk University Library.*

❖ A DIVERSE THEATER SCENE

Live theatrical performances offered audiences a wide variety of entertainment experiences during the 1900s. The Broadway Theater district in New York City, which was known as "The Great White Way," was the focal point of the American theatrical world. Its artistic merits, however, were not as brilliant as its electrical marquees. Broadway theater consisted largely of sentimental melodramas lavishly produced but weak on plot and character. The New York audiences of the 1900s were middle class, conservative, and reluctant to be disturbed by plots based on real-life social ills. To be successful, a play had to have a big-name star and refrain from displaying vulgar language and risqué situations. Commercial theater productions, which by 1900 were financed almost entirely by a centralized business trust known as the Theatrical Syndicate, were happy to accommodate the audience's demand for style over substance.

Theatrical performances were not limited solely to Broadway, however. Vaudeville shows were attended by members of all economic classes and appeared—via theatrical chains known as circuits—in nearly every town across in the country. Vaudeville shows consisted of jugglers, animal acts, acrobats, magicians, skits, recitations, comics, and ventriloquists. Many popular performers of film, radio, and television got their start in vaudeville.

During the first decade of the twentieth century ethnic and racial stereotyping was common and most minority cultures were presented on stage with something less than dignity. It is not surprising that "The Great White Way" was white in more ways than one in the early 1900s. Although white actors frequently put on black-face makeup to play comedic parts, African American performers were not often seen. Still, some black actors were able to break through the theater's wall of prejudice and become stars. Among them was Bert Williams (1874–1922), who starred in *In Dahomey* (1903), the first full-length Broadway musical written and performed by African Americans. Other minorities faced similar difficulties on the stage. Asians and Hispanics were virtually nonexistent on Broadway. Other popular theaters catered to immigrant audiences in their native tongues.

Dance was also a lively art form during the 1900s. Like theater, a puritanical sense of decency and decorum had kept dancing under strict control. Americans in general did not appreciate expressive movement of the body. Dance was considered a "common" amusement by the upper classes, and the public dance halls in the first decade of the 1900s were most decidedly of the common sort.

❖ THE DUELING WORLDS OF JOURNALISM

American journalism at the turn of the century had evolved into two distinct camps. The first, symbolized by *The New York Times*, followed a

Tin Pan Alley

The term "Tin Pan Alley" was coined in 1903 to describe the area of New York City on Twenty-Eighth Street between Broadway and Sixth Avenue where a jumble of sounds could be heard from every window, while composers pounded on their pianos in search of a hit song. The goal of Tin Pan Alley musicians was to draft a popular song that could be sold nationally as sheet music. The composers attracted a national audience by celebrating current events and popular pastimes through song. Among the best known songs to come from Tin Pan Alley: "Take Me Out to the Ball Game" (1908), "Mary's a Grand Old Name" (1905), "School Days" (1907), and "Why Did I Pick a Lemon in the Garden of Love?" (1909). These and other catchy novelty songs spread across America on sheet music and through performances by "pluggers," singers employed by music publishers to sell the tunes to live audiences.

strict policy of printing only the facts. It took a dispassionate tone and aspired to strict objectivity in its reporting. Its readers, largely people from the upper middle class, needed accurate information to run their businesses and they enjoyed the paper's cultured tone. The second style, known as the New Journalism or yellow journalism, targeted a much broader audience of urban workers. Papers such as Joseph Pulitzer's *New York World* and William Randolph Hearst's *New York Journal* sought to entertain their readers with stories rather than to inform them with strictly reported facts.

Between 1895 and 1905 the comic strip evolved into a new art form and newspaper feature. Gradual improvements in color printing presses led publishers, in their attempts to boost circulation, to introduce color supplements in their Sunday editions. Among the most popular comic strips were *Hogan's Alley, The Yellow Kid, Buster Brown,* and *The Katzenjammer Kids.* The most significant of these was *The Yellow Kid* by Richard Outcault (1863–1928). The character, a bald young boy who wore a large yellow nightshirt, became a cultural phenomenon and soon appeared on a flood of merchandise. The boy's nightshirt was also the source of the term "yellow journalism," which was given to the era of newspaper publishing characterized by the rivalry of the Pulitzer and Hearst chains.

BOOKS

Alter, Judy. *Vaudeville: The Birth of Show Business*. New York: Franklin Watts, Inc., 1998.

Blum, Daniel; enlarged by John Willis. *A Pictorial History of the American Theatre*. 6th edition. New York: Crown Publishers, 1986.

Chocolate, Deborah M. N. *The Piano Man*. New York: Walker & Company, 1998.

Cohen, Daniel. *Yellow Journalism: Scandal, Sensationalism and Gossip in the Media*. Brookfield, CT: Twenty-First Century Books, 2000.

Dwight, Eleanor. *Edith Wharton: An Extraordinary Life*. New York: Harry N. Abrams, 1999.

Dyer, Daniel. *Jack London: A Biography*. New York: Scholastic Press, 1997.

Fleming, Thomas. *Behind the Headlines: The Story of American Newspapers*. New York: Walker, 1989.

Frazier, Nancy. *William Randolph Hearst: Modern Media Tycoon*. New York: Blackbriar Marketing, 2001.

Furia, Philip. *The Poets of Tin Pan Alley: A History of America's Great Lyricists*. New York: Oxford University Press, 1992.

Galf, Jackie. *1900–1920: The Birth of Modernism*. New York: Gareth Stevens, 2000.

Isadora, Rachel. *Isadora Dances*. New York: Puffin, 2000.

Janson, H.W., and Anthony F. Janson. *History of Art for Young People,* 5th edition. New York: Harry Abrams, 1997.

Leach, William, and Matina Homer. *Edith Wharton*. New York: Chelsea House Publishers, 1987.

Lisandrelli, Elaine. *Jack London: A Writer's Adventurous Life*. Springfield, NJ: Ensloe Publishers, 1999.

Otfinoski, Steven. *Scott Joplin: A Life in Ragtime*. New York: Franklin & Watts, 1995.

Phillips, Julien. *Stars of the Ziegfeld Follies*. Minneapolis: Lerner Publishers, 1972.

Slide, Anthony. *Early American Cinema*. New York: A. S. Barnes, 1970.

Streissguth, Thomas. *Mary Cassatt: Portrait of an American Impressionist*. Minneapolis: Carolrhoda, 1998.

WEB SITES

Media History Timeline: 1900s. http://www.mediahistory.umn.edu/time/1900s.html (accessed on August 8, 2002).

Modern Art Timeline. http://notaflag.com/timeline.htm (accessed on August 8, 2002).

The 1900s: 1900–1909. http://archer2000.tripod.com/1900.html (accessed on August 8, 2002).

Southern Music in the Twentieth Century. http://www.southernmusic.net/1900.htm (accessed on August 8, 2002).

chapter two   *Business and
the Economy*

1900: March 14 Congress passes the Gold Standard Act to improve the national economy. The act established that all U.S. currency was backed by and exchangeable for gold.

1900: March 31 The first national advertisement for automobiles appears in *The Saturday Evening Post*.

1900: September 17 The newly formed United Mine Workers (UMW) union stages its first strike in Pennsylvania with nearly 100,000 miners participating.

1901: January 10 The oil gusher known as Spindletop blasts near Beaumont, Texas, establishing the petroleum industry in the Lone Star State.

1901: February 25 Formed by a merger of ten companies, U.S. Steel is established as the world's largest industrial corporation.

1902: May 12 The UMW stages a strike against the coal industry, demanding union representation, wage increases, and eight-hour workdays. Known as the "Anthracite Coal Strike," this labor action lasts five months and endangers the nation's economy.

1902: June 1 The state of Maryland passes the nation's first worker's compensation law to protect workers injured on the job.

1902: June 17 The National Reclamation Act is passed by Congress, authorizing the federal government to build dams in the West for irrigation.

1903: February 14 The Department of Commerce and Labor is created at the cabinet level by Congress to regulate and organize business activity.

1903: November 30 The U.S. Supreme Court rules in *Atkin* v. *Kansas* that an eight-hour workday for public works construction workers is constitutional.

1903: December 17 In Kitty Hawk, North Carolina, Wilbur and Orville Wright make their first sustained flight, setting the stage for the development of the airline industry.

1904: April 30 The World's Fair, called the Louisiana Purchase Exposition, begins in St. Louis, Missouri.

1904: October 27 The New York City subway opens, becoming the country's first rapid transit system.

1905: February 23 The Rotary Club, the nation's first business-related service organization, is founded in Chicago.

1905: June 27 The Industrial Workers of the World (IWW) is created as a nationwide industrial union. Known as the "Wobblies," the IWW seeks to unite all industrial workers in a union.

1905: **December 30** Former Idaho governor Frank Steunenberg is murdered by a bomb explosion. Law enforcement officials accuse prominent union organizers of the crime. The case becomes one of the most notorious labor trials of the century.

1906: **April 18** San Francisco sustains a major earthquake and subsequent fire, which destroy much of the city. The devastation leaves 250,000 people homeless, 25,000 buildings destroyed, and 500 dead.

1906: **June 30** Congress passes the Pure Food and Drug Act, prohibiting the mislabeling or contamination of food involved in interstate and foreign commerce.

1906: **July 22** The last U.S. cable car stops running in Chicago.

1907: **March 13** A sharp stock market drop sparks a financial panic, which in turn leads to unemployment, high food prices, and bank failures.

1907: **July 29** William "Big Bill" D. Haywood is found not guilty in the murder of former Idaho governor Frank Steunenberg. The real killer confesses and is revealed

to be working for the Mine Owners' Association, which planted the bomb in order to frame union organizers.

1907: **October 21** A run on the Knickerbocker Trust Company in New York City starts a string of bank and trust failures. The U.S. Treasury and private banker J. P. Morgan step in to provide money to end the financial panic.

1907: **December** A total of six hundred coal miners die in explosions in Jacobs Creek, Pennsylvania, and Monongah, West Virginia.

1908: **July 26** The forerunner to the Federal Bureau of Investigation (FBI) is established. The agency is formed to investigate organized labor, fight the greed of big business, and prevent the theft of public lands.

1908: **October 1** The Ford Motor Company unveils the Model T automobile. The $825 price tag makes it possible for people with moderate incomes to purchase an automobile.

1909: **July 12** The Sixteenth Amendment to the Constitution, authorizing income taxes, is authorized by Congress.

1909: **November 22** A three-month strike by the International Ladies' Garment Workers Union begins in New York, with twenty thousand U. S. garment workers participating.

Overview

America's business and economic sectors changed dramatically during the first decade of the twentieth century. Agriculture, which had been the nation's primary employer throughout the previous century, was gradually being replaced by industry. The United States was expanding its economic interests around the globe and emerging as a world power. This business expansion meant increased wealth as raw materials became cheaper to obtain, driving prices down and consumption up. Among the most prosperous businesses of the era were the oil, steel, textile, railroad, and food production industries. The decade was further marked by major technological innovations, such as the birth of the automobile and aviation industries. Americans who entered the century riding horse-drawn buggies could, by the end of its first decade, drive cars and dream of someday flying in a plane.

Many of the workers who were employed by the nation's expanding industrial base were immigrants. Nearly nine million immigrants journeyed to America during the decade, with most arrivals coming from Italy, Austria-Hungary, and Russia. The record year for immigration was 1907, when 1.29 million people entered the United States. By the end of the decade, the U.S. population had risen to 91 million. Men and women rarely competed for jobs, primarily because of division of labor according to gender. In the industrial sector, men had opportunities and could claim jobs that required physical strength, while women were confined to low-paying jobs using light machinery. Although by 1910 one-third of the workforce was female, half of these women workers were involved in agriculture or domestic service, leaving little female representation in industry. Children were often exploited as workers. Until regulation ended the practice, child labor was common. In 1900 more than 250,000 children under the age of fifteen worked in factories for minimal pay. Average union wages in 1900 were thirty-four cents per hour, compared to non-union, unskilled pay of fifteen cents per hour. The average workweek in the decade was fifty-three hours. Unskilled laborers especially faced many difficulties, since their income would not support a family of five even if they worked twelve hours a day every day of the year.

The century began with businesses expanding by merging with similar companies (horizontal integration) and taking on additional functions in the production and sale of their products (vertical integration). The result was the elimination of competition. Many Americans became concerned about the continued rise of big business through trusts, trade associations, cartels, or pools. They feared that these business groups would destroy America's image as the land of opportunity where it was possible for an individual to succeed through his or her own business efforts.

The 1900s witnessed the founding of numerous corporations that have since become fixtures in American life: Firestone Tire and Rubber Company (1900), United States Steel Company (1901), Quaker Oats Company (1901), J.C. Penney Company (1902), Pepsi-Cola Company (1902), Texaco (1903), Harley-Davidson (1907), Hershey (1908), and General Motors Corporation (1908). The general prosperity of the decade made many Americans eager consumers, especially as companies began to spend more time and money on product advertising.

The rise of big business and poor working conditions for common laborers led to increased tensions between employers and employees. Throughout the decade many workers joined organized labor unions, but their efforts to improve pay and workplace conditions were often unsuccessful. Several long and violent strikes occurred during the 1900s, and some of these work stoppages required government intervention to resolve the disputes. The great differences in the lifestyles of owners and workers was highly publicized, notably through the Anthracite Coal Strike. Nevertheless, union power became increasingly fragmented as worker unity was lost amid internal divisions based on race, gender, nationality, skill, and political beliefs.

Although the 1900s had a generally optimistic economic outlook, the confidence of many Americans was shaken by the sharp stock market drop in 1907. The first sign of financial panic was a run on the Knickerbocker Trust Company of New York, which collapsed the banking and credit system. Confidence was restored because of the actions of the U.S. Treasury along with capitalists under the leadership of J.P. Morgan, who stabilized the banks and corporations with their own funds. Despite the gap between America's rich and poor, the first decade of the century brought increasing commercialism to the lives of all Americans.

Andrew Carnegie (1835–1919) Scottish industrialist Andrew Carnegie became one of America's wealthiest men during the nineteenth century. By the 1870s his Carnegie Steel Corporation dominated the industry. He sold his majority holdings in the corporation in 1901 for $250 million. Believing that the rich had a duty to distribute their surplus wealth for the betterment of civilization, Carnegie became a philanthropist. He had given away 90 percent of his fortune by the time of his death, mostly to benefit educational institutions and to establish free public libraries. *Photograph reproduced by permission of AP/Wide World Photos.*

Eugene V. Debs (1855–1926) Indiana native Eugene V. Debs was a tireless union organizer and a spokesperson on labor issues. In 1881, Debs was elected national secretary of the Brotherhood of Locomotive Firemen. He gained national attention during the 1894 strike against the Pullman Company when federal troops arrested Debs and other labor leaders. Debs soon embraced socialism as the answer to the workers' problems. Between 1900 and 1920 Debs was the Socialist Party's candidate in five presidential elections. While many workers admired Debs' vision, relatively few endorsed his political agenda. *Photograph courtesy of the Library of Congress.*

Henry Ford (1863–1947) Industrialist Henry Ford pioneered production techniques that allowed for the high-volume manufacture of automobiles at low cost. His methods allowed middle- and working-class Americans to purchase their first cars and helped him build the first of the giant car companies. The Ford Motor Company was incorporated in 1903 and quickly prospered by building autos more efficiently and selling them more cheaply than other automakers. Between 1908 and 1927, Ford sold more than fifteen million Model T's, or "Tin Lizzies."

William "Big Bill" D. Haywood (1869–1928) Labor leader William "Big Bill" D. Haywood gained national attention in 1906 when he was jailed for his alleged involvement in the murder of former Idaho governor Frank Steunenberg. Haywood was later acquitted of the murder charge. Haywood became a leader of the Socialist Party of America and urged workers to practice sabotage and foster a revolution. He assumed control of the Industrial Workers of the World (IWW) union in 1911. In 1917, he and other IWW leaders were found guilty of espionage and of violating the Sedition Act during World War I (1914–18). While released on bail, Haywood fled to the Soviet Union and lived the remainder of his life in exile. *Photograph courtesy of the Library of Congress.*

Andrew William Mellon (1855–1937) Banker and financier Andrew William Mellon was one of the most important American capitalists during the first decade of the twentieth century. He honed his financial expertise while working at his father's banking house. Mellon built his own fortune by shrewdly judging businesses and constantly reinvesting profits in well-run businesses. Mellon provided many young companies with the capital they needed to become dominant, including the Aluminum Company of America (Alcoa), the Gulf Oil Corporation, and the Union Steel Company. In later life, Mellon became active in Republican politics and was a noted philanthropist. President Warren G. Harding appointed him Secretary of the Treasury. *Photograph reproduced by permission of Archive Photos, Inc.*

J. Pierpont Morgan (1837–1913) Banker J. Pierpont. Morgan headed J. P. Morgan and Company, the most important force in American finance in the quarter-century before World War I. Born into a wealthy family, Morgan turned his family's banking house into one of the most prosperous in the world. In 1901, he purchased Andrew Carnegie's steel interests, merging them with his own to form the world's largest company: the United States Steel Corporation. He was also involved in the formation of General Electric and International Harvester. Morgan was seen by many as the symbol of concentrated economic power or "trusts." *Photograph reproduced by permission of Archive Photos, Inc.*

James Cash Penney (1875–1971) James Cash (J.C.) Penney became convinced that a chain of a department stores would be successful in 1899, when T. M. Callahan, a dry goods merchant, offered Penney the opportunity to purchase a one-third partnership in his Wyoming store. By 1907, Penney owned forty-eight stores across the country, with headquarters in New York City. His chain continued to expand so quickly that Penney opened an average of one new store every ten days for forty years. At his death, Penney's chain was the second-largest nonfood retailer in the country, after Sears, Roebuck and Company. *Photograph courtesy of the Library of Congress.*

Charles Michael Schwab (1862–1939) Charles Michael Schwab began his career in the steel industry as an engineer's helper at the Thomson Steel Works during the 1880s. He rapidly rose within the Carnegie-owned company by using his management skills to solve labor disputes and public relations problems. In 1897, he was appointed president of the Carnegie Steel Company. Schwab purchased a controlling interest in the Bethlehem Steel Company in 1901 and merged it with U.S. Shipbuilding. Schwab built the company into U.S. Steel's greatest rival. Unsound investments late in his life led to the depletion of his fortune. He died insolvent in 1939. *Photograph courtesy of the Library of Congress.*

❖ ANTHRACITE COAL STRIKE OF 1902

America's transformation from an agricultural to an industrial economy was marked by great tensions between business owners and their employees. One of the most significant of these disputes was the Anthracite Coal Strike, which nearly crippled the American economic system. Led by John Mitchell (1870–1919), president of the United Mine Workers (UMW) , 150,000 miners began their strike on May 12, 1902, to demand better wages, a shorter workday, and union recognition. The strike dragged on for nearly a year as the two sides failed to reach an agreement and the nation's coal supply dwindled to dangerously low levels. The effects of the work stoppage were felt beyond the mines as the price of coal, which was five dollars per ton when the strike began, spiraled upward to reach thirty dollars per ton by the strike's end. As the price of coal rose, businesses and schools closed to conserve fuel, and raids on railroad cars carrying the precious cargo began to occur.

President Theodore Roosevelt (1858–1919) tried to intervene in the strike and bring about a settlement that would be acceptable to both the mine owners and their workers. In September 1902, Roosevelt called for government representatives to meet with both labor and management and reach an agreement. The president's plan was to offer both sides an equal voice in resolving the matter. He was concerned that coal shortages during the winter would be harmful to the nation's citizens and economy. In an address to both sides he stated, "I appeal to your patriotism, to the spirit that sinks personal consideration and makes individual sacrifices for the general good."

John Mitchell of the UMW agreed with the president's words and asked him to appoint a commission to settle the strike. Mitchell further said that the union would accept the commission's decision if the owners would. The owners, however, refused to negotiate. They called the unionists "anarchists" (people in favor of political disorder) and suggested that Roosevelt direct the military to end the strike. The conference led Roosevelt to believe that the mine operators might be at fault in the strike, and the public echoed this sentiment when news of the conference hit the press. The American people were sympathetic toward the miners. A week after the conference, Roosevelt announced his intentions to threaten the mine operators into a settlement by having the mines run by the army, which would, in effect, remove the owners from their own businesses.

In October, Roosevelt announced the creation of a special commission comprised of members from various professions, and the strike was called

George F. Baer, president of the Reading (pronounced RED-ing) Railroad and spokesman for mine operators, best expressed the attitude of the mine owners toward their employees. In response to a letter asking the Holy Spirit to send "reason to [Baer's] heart," Baer revealed the operators' scorn and contempt for the miners in what has come to be known as the "divine right letter":

My dear Mr. Clark:

I have your letter of the 16th instant.

I do not know who you are. I see that you are a religious man, but you are evidently biased in favor of the right of the working man to control a business in which he has no other interest than to secure fair wages for the work he does.

I beg you not to be discouraged. The right and interests of the laboring man will be protected and cared for—not by labor agitators, but by the Christian men to whom God in his infinite wisdom has given the control of the property interests of the country, and upon the successful Management of which so much depends.

Do not be discouraged. Pray earnestly that right may triumph, always remembering that the Lord God Omnipotent still reigns, and that His reign is one of law and order, and not of violence and crime.

off. Mediation began in November and continued for five months. During the trial-like proceedings, more than 558 witnesses were called on the part of labor, nonunion labor, the operators, and the commission. The owners argued it was their right to do as they pleased with their businesses. Representing the UMW was famed attorney Clarence Darrow (1857–1938), who questioned the operators' "God-given right to hire the cheapest man they can get." The mediation ended in March 1903, with the union accepting a 10 percent pay increase and a nine-hour day. President Roosevelt was given much credit for his role in ending the strike, and his intervention became one of the most celebrated actions of his presidency.

❖ **THE FINANCIAL PANIC OF 1907**

The relatively prosperous first years of the 1900s came to an end in 1907. Drains on the U.S. money supply revealed a weak national financial structure of banking and credit, causing an economic crisis that lasted for nearly a year. The low money supply was partially caused by a lack of cash flow from farmers due to a late growing season. It was further drained by overly speculative investing in copper, money diverted to fund the Russo-Japanese War of 1905, the costly rebuilding of San Francisco after the devastating 1906 earthquake, and the national railroad expansion program. In March, the stock market fell dramatically, and soon thereafter prices soared, wages dropped, unemployment rose, and many banks and businesses failed. The first financial institution to fall into trouble was Mercantile National Bank. Because there was no central banking system to aid troubled financial institutions, the bank sought assistance from the Clearing House Association, a banking agency that cleared checks. When the Clearing House Association investigated the bank, they declared it to be solvent, or financially sound, but the panic had already begun.

J. P. Morgan, a leader of America's financial community, was concerned the panic surrounding Mercantile National might affect the already weakening American economy. He soon directed that a team of trusted financial advisors be assembled to work toward a solution. Among those on the team were Thomas W. Joyce of the House of Morgan, Richard Trimble of the United States Steel Corporation, Henry P. Davidson of First National Bank, and Benjamin Strong of Bankers Trust Company. Much of the financial team's concern focused on the Knickerbocker Trust Company of New York, the third largest bank in New York City. Depositors had begun a "run" on the bank, demanding all their funds be removed from the bank. Financial ruin loomed for Knickerbocker when it was revealed that only 5 percent of the bank's deposits were held in reserve (available for immediate withdrawal by depositors). The bank president, who was forced to resign, suffered a nervous breakdown and committed suicide within weeks. Soon, the panic spread throughout the city.

Morgan's financial interventions with other capitalists and an infusion of funds from the U.S. Treasury eventually eased the panic. Confidence was ultimately restored, though it took several weeks before the crisis was ended. Despite some failures, in the end twelve financial institutions that had been on the verge of collapse were saved. Fortunately, no large banks failed.

The financial crisis of 1907 was so severe, however, that changes in the national economic structure were designed to prevent future panics. Congress passed laws that regulated how banks could issues bonds (a certificate of debt that pays interest), such as the Aldrich-Vreeland Act of 1908. The National Monetary Commission was also established in 1908. It served as a forerunner to the Federal Reserve Bank, which effectively centralized the

America's dependence upon coal was eased with the discovery of the Spindletop oil gusher in Beaumont, Texas, in 1901. The gusher established the petroleum industry in Texas, where 491 oil companies were operating by the next year. The company formed around the find was initially called Guffey Oil after Colonel J. M. Guffey, one of its financiers. The name was change to Gulf Oil in 1907 after Guffey was implicated in a financial scandal. The gusher was international news, and the well eventually produced more than 100,000 gallons of oil per day.

banking industry in 1913. The economic restructuring that resulted from the Panic of 1907 was crucial to solidifying American's economic foundation so that it could emerge as a world financial power in the coming years.

❖ THE WOBBLIES

The Industrial Workers of the World (IWW), a national industrial union, was established in Chicago in 1905. Union leaders from across the country hoped to accomplish on a national scale what the Western Federation of Miners (WFM) had done for mining labor. The IWW advocated "syndicalism," a revolutionary worker-controlled society. It recruited workers regardless of job skill, race, or gender. The goal of "one big union" for all industrial workers was the primary aim of the IWW. At its peak in 1912, the IWW had 60,000 members, with its most active participants involved in mining, construction, lumber, textiles, and migratory agriculture. The IWW declined due to competing factions within its membership. The IWW promoted the idea that capitalists were the enemy of the working class.

❖ THE LABOR TRIAL OF THE CENTURY

One of the most infamous court cases of the early twentieth century was the trial of William "Big Bill" D. Haywood for the murder of former Idaho governor Frank Steunenberg. The former governor was killed on December 30, 1905, by a bomb that had been rigged to the gate in front of his home. There were no witnesses to the crime. The state and Steunenberg's family offered a reward of $15,000 for the murderer's capture. James McPharlan, chief of the famed Pinkerton Security firm, an established strikebreaking organization, headed up the investigation.

Governor Steunenberg had originally been a pro-union politician. He was condemned by union members when, however, he called for federal troops to face down the Western Federation of Miners (WFM) after an uprising at a mine in 1899. Union members were imprisoned for months and remained bitter toward Steunenberg. Soon a man named Harry Orchard appeared and announced his knowledge of vital information regarding the crime. He was arrested on January 1, 1906, and reportedly endured ten days of intense grilling by McPharlan before he confessed to the killing. Orchard said members of the WFM's "inner circle" paid him $250 to kill Steunenberg. In reality, Orchard was a spy working for the mine operators. He falsely accused William "Big Bill" D. Haywood, secretary of the WFM; Charles Moyer, president of the WFM; and George Pettibone, a blacklisted miner of the murder. Together Orchard and McPharlan created the false details of the crime as they worked to discredit the union. The accused men were jailed for months in the death house of an Idaho prison.

The trial was a national sensation. Ironically, public sympathy for the accused unionists grew after President Theodore Roosevelt called the three WFM members "undesirable citizens."

Soon, thousands of union supporters wore placards that read "I am an undesirable citizen." Boise came to be known as "Murdertown" because of the local industry that sprung up around the trial.

Haywood's defense was aided when his noted attorney, Clarence Darrow, got Orchard to confess that he had lied in previous trials and had in the past confessed to crimes that he never committed. After a three-month trial, Haywood was found not guilty. Moyer and Pettibone were also later cleared of the charges. The trial's most significant result was that many other crimes blamed on union members were revealed to be ploys by operators to discredit the union. Though he had committed other crimes for the Mine Owners' Association, killing Frank Steunenberg was Orchard's own idea. The mine owners' willingness to take part in Orchard's lies left them disgraced. The public was shocked at the revelations and gave the unions much-needed support in their efforts to improve labor conditions.

OPPOSITE PAGE
Child laborers, working the textile mills. Child labor was common even after the first child labor law was passed in 1908.
Courtesy of the Library of Congress.

❖ LIMITING BUSINESS

During the post-Civil War period, the federal government's legislative and judicial branches allowed the business community's actions to remain unregulated. At the turn of the century, however, the government began to

Roosevelt's "Square Deal"

. . . .

President Theodore Roosevelt attempted to provide all sectors of the economy—business, labor, and the public—a voice in the nation's financial matters. The "Square Deal" platform from his 1904 presidential campaign called for an even-handed, fair approach to all parties involved in business-related matters. Its great flaw was that it promised only an abstract notion of fairness.

dramatically reverse its "hands off" policy. The years 1900 to 1909 witnessed many landmark pieces of congressional legislation and Supreme Court rulings, which more strongly controlled the nation's business and economic interests. Congress enacted laws to correct the abuses that had occurred in such areas as fiscal policy, labor unrest, the quality of consumer goods, and the unregulated power of large corporate trusts. Congress' goal during the 1900s was to restore the public's confidence in the economy and the goods and services traded within it. Nine of the most important legislative acts of the period are described below.

Congress passed the Gold Standard Act (1900) in order to establish national banks in rural communities with populations fewer than 3,000 people. These banks were designed to support agricultural growth. Furthermore, the act created a stable national currency, which was vital to the United States in expanding its role in international commerce.

The Elkins Act (1903) prohibited railroads from changing their published rates. Many of the country's products were transported by rail, and this piece of legislation regulated interstate commerce.

The Expedition Act (1903) was strongly promoted by President Theodore Roosevelt as an important piece of antitrust legislation. It allowed antitrust lawsuits to move more quickly through the judicial system.

The Heyburn Bill (1906) is considered the nation's first consumer protection law. The bill regulated the United States's food supply by requiring product labeling and outlawing the sale of diseased, decomposing, or contaminated meats and other foodstuffs.

The Hepburn Act (1906), also known as the Railway Rate Regulation Act, overhauled the Interstate Commerce Act of 1887. The Hepburn Act gave the

Teddy Roosevelt and the Teddy Bear

During a 1902 hunting trip in Mississippi, President Theodore Roosevelt failed to shoot any game. Several of his supporters did not wish to see the president disappointed, and they arranged to have a bear cub placed on Roosevelt's path so he could kill it. However, Roosevelt refused to shoot an animal in such an unsportsmanlike manner. The press reported the incident and the president's encounter with the cub made national headlines. Clifford K. Berryman depicted Roosevelt's actions in an editorial cartoon in *The Washington Post* on November 16, 1902. The cartoon was titled "Drawing the Line in Mississippi" and had a double meaning. Not only did it comment on Roosevelt's drawing the line on sportsmanship but it also referred to his settlement of a boundary dispute between Louisiana and Mississippi while on the trip. Soon, Morris and Rose Mitchom of Brooklyn, New York, who ran a candy store, obtained permission from the president to use his nickname "Teddy" on a brown bear with movable body parts. The original toy was hand-stitched by Rose and called "Teddy's Bear." Later, the name was shortened to "Teddy Bear." Within a year a teddy bear craze had gripped the nation. The teddy bear remained a popular childhood toy through the century.

Interstate Commerce Commission (ICC) greater powers to investigate the railroad trusts, which were infamous for their questionable business practices. Its most powerful effect was allowing the ICC to regulate railroad rates.

The Meat Inspection Act (1906) was designed to improve the horrible conditions of the meatpacking industry. It dictated that there must be regular federal inspections of all meat products traded through interstate and foreign commerce.

The Pure Food and Drug Act (1906) made it illegal to mislabel or tamper with foods involved in interstate or foreign commerce. This law and The Meat Inspection Act combined to become the strongest regulations ever imposed upon the food industry.

The Aldrich-Vreeland Act (1908) corrected problems in the nation's banking system. It allowed banks to issue bonds based on the securities of other bonds, but imposed a 10 percent tax on those notes.

The Payne-Aldrich Tariff Act (1909) lowered tariffs (taxes imposed on imported or exported goods) for some specific sectors of the economy, such as the shoe production industry. This law caused great controversy because some industries, like iron and steel, were angered that their tariffs were not lowered while others, like those in the silk and cotton industries, actually were raised.

At the beginning of the twentieth century large business monopolies, or trusts, had become powerful economic forces as they concentrated their fiscal power and squeezed out their small business rivals. Trusts did have some positive qualities, such as creating higher production capacity and reducing the duplication of effort. However, these economic savings were not always passed on to the stockholder, laborers, or the consumer. With Theodore Roosevelt's rise to the presidency the antitrust movement gained momentum. To Roosevelt, "good trusts" benefited the public by bringing new capital and products into the economy. "Bad trusts" consisted of greedy financiers interested only in earning profits at the public's expense. Roosevelt led the charge to prosecute and break up bad trusts.

Congress and the President were aided in their regulatory efforts by the Supreme Court, which decided many cases affecting business through the decade. Some of the high court's most important cases heard during the first decade of the twentieth century are described below.

Atkin v. *Kansas* (1903). The Court ruled that a Kansas law establishing an eight-hour workday for construction workers involved in public works was not a violation of "freedom of contract" as provided for in the Constitution.

Northern Securities v. *United States* (1904) held that the merger of the Northern Pacific, Great Northern, and Burlington Railroads violated the Sherman Antitrust Act. This decision was vital to strengthening President Roosevelt's trust-busting policies.

The Roosevelt administration's antitrust policies were especially helped by the case of *Hale* v. *Henkel* (1906), which ruled that employees called as witnesses in antitrust cases can be forced to testify and provide evidence against their employers.

❖ CHANGING THE WAY AMERICANS BUILT PRODUCTS

New methods of manufacture revolutionized several industries during the decade. When Henry Ford (1863–1947) introduced the Model T automobile (nicknamed the "Tin Lizzie"), he said it was a "motor car for the great multitudes." Ford was correct, and the success of the Model T ushered the United States into the automobile age. The Model T's greatest innovation was not the car itself, but instead the way it was manufactured. Using ideas developed by Frederick Taylor (1856–1915), Ford developed the use of the assembly line. In previous decades, factory workers moved from product to product in order to perform their duties. At Ford factories, the workers did not move from car to car. Instead, the parts to be assembled into an automobile were placed on a conveyor belt, which moved as the workers stood in their places. The moving assembly line revolutionized car production and was soon transplanted to other manufacturing businesses. Ford's use of the moving assembly line is hailed as one of the major accomplishments of the Industrial Revolution. The mass production of the Model T allowed the car to be sold at a price that was affordable to many Americans who had never before been able to purchase a car. Within only a few years, American culture was transformed as people became more mobile.

Another manufacturing innovation relied on the research of Frederick Taylor. Named for its creator, Taylorism attempted to make a science out of work-related tasks by defining the one best way to do any given job. Taylor used scientific methods of observation and recording to determine the most efficient ways to accomplish a task. Among his recommendations were to scientifically select and train workers, monitor their work progress, and give greater responsibilities to management. The result of Taylor's philosophy was that workers were obligated to match the speed of the machinery they used. Taylorism was seen by many business leaders as

*An assembly line at Ford Motor Company, where workers produced the Model T. **Reproduced by permission of AP/Wide World Photos.***

a positive force for it often increased production quotas by as much as 200 percent.

Businesses that followed Taylor's principles saw their profits increase enormously, and the United States came to be seen as nation with some of the world's most efficient production methods. However, Taylorism was also strongly criticized for having a dehumanizing effect on labor, as workers were thought of as little more than cogs in a machine. It resulted in a great division of the workforce: Management became the "thinkers" in a corporation and had absolute control over their employees; workers became the "doers" whose jobs required little intellectual skill as they performed routine exercises over and over.

❖ ADVERTISING AND THE RISE OF POPULAR AMERICAN BRANDS

A production line at the Krupp steel mills.
Reproduced by permission of Foto Marburg/Art Resource.

Advertising grew increasingly important during the 1900s as companies sought ways to attract consumers' attention. One of the most success-

ful and long-lasting advertising campaigns in American history emerged in 1904 when the Campbell's Soup Company introduced the cute Campbell's Kids on their packaging. Created by artist Grace Widerseim to appeal to women, the chubby cartoon boy and girl were modified only slightly in later decades. Product spin-offs featuring the adorable duo have included dozens of novelty toys and household items. Campbell was one of the first corporations to understand that creating a likable image or character to represent a product is an effective way to attract consumers.

Another consumer product that became established in the 1900s was Pepsi-Cola. Developed by drugstore owner Caleb D. Bradham in 1898, the original soda was designed to compete with the many popular kola nut drinks on the market, especially Coca-Cola. Initially called "Brad's Drink" by Bradham's friends, it was renamed "Pepsi-Cola" for its alleged pharmaceutical properties. Bradham claimed the soda relieved dyspepsia, today called indigestion. Early ads for the soda promoted its supposed healthful benefits: "Pepsi-Cola: At Soda Fountains. Exhilarating. Invigorating. Aids Digestion."

. . . . *For More Information*

BOOKS

Bartoletti, Susan Campbell. *Growing Up in Coal Country*. New York: Houghton Mifflin, 1999.

Bartoletti, Susan Campbell. *Kids on Strike!* New York: Houghton Mifflin, 1999.

Byman, Jeremy. *J.P. Morgan: Banker to a Growing Nation*. New York: Morgan Reynolds, 2001.

Freedman, Russell, and Lewis Hine. *Kids at Work: Lewis Hine and the Crusade Against Child Labor*. New York: Clarion Books, 1998.

Fritz, Jean, and Mike Wimmer. *Bully for You, Teddy Roosevelt!* New York: Paper Star Paperbacks, 1999.

Gibbons, Faye. *Mama and Me and the Model T*. New York: Morrow Junior, 1999.

Gourley, Catherine. *Wheels of Time: A Biography of Henry Ford*. New York: Millbrook Press, 1997.

Guthridge, Sue, and Wallace Wook. *Thomas Edison: Young Inventor*. New York: Aladdin Paperbacks, 1988.

Meltzer, Milton: *Bread and Roses: The Struggle of American Labor, 1865–1915*. New York, Knopf, 1967.

Murphy, Frank. *The Legend of the Teddy Bear*. New York: Sleeping Bear Press, 2000.

O'Connell, Arthur J. *American Business in the 20th Century*. San Mateo, CA: Bluewood Books, 1999.

Simon, Charman. *Andrew Carnegie: Builder of Libraries*. New York: Children's Press, 1998.

Stevenson, Augusta, and Robert Dormies. *Wilbur and Orville Wright: Young Fliers*. New York: Aladdin Paperbacks, 1986.

Sullivan, Otha Richard, and James Haskins. *African American Inventors*. New York: John Wiley & Sons, 1998.

WEB SITES

Alexandria Archaeology Museum—Discovering the Decades: 1900s. http://oha.ci. alexandria.va.us/archaeology/decades/ar-decades-1900.html (accessed on August 8, 2002).

The Campaign to End Child Labor. http://www.boondocksnet.com/labor (accessed on August 8, 2002).

Joe Hill: Early 1900s Labor. http://www.pbs.org/joehill/early/index.html (accessed on August 8, 2002).

The 1900s: 1900–1909. http://archer2000.tripod.com/1900.html (accessed on August 8, 2002).

Telecom History—The Early 1900s. http://www.webconsult.com/1900.html (accessed on August 8, 2002).

chapter three *Education*

1900: **March** School baths are planned for students in some schools by the New York City School Board of Education.

1900: **May 12** The College Entrance Examination Board is created.

1900: **July 11** There is "art in everything," asserts progressive educator Francis Parker in a speech pleading for the centrality of art in education before the National Education Association.

1900: **September 15** Lack of space forces the Atlanta, Georgia, school system to turn away four hundred students.

1901: **January** Bryn Mawr University President M. Carey Thomas supports the equality of college education for both men and women in an article in *Educational Review*.

1901: **June** The College Board's entrance examination is given to high school students for the first time.

1901: **June 12** Students of Bunsen School in Belleville, Illinois, strike in an effort to shorten their school day.

1901: **November 4** The reform-minded Southern Education Board meets for the first time.

1901: **December** Steel tycoon Andrew Carnegie endows a science research center, the Carnegie Institution of Washington, with a gift of $10 million.

1902: **July** Emory University Professor Andrew Stedd attacks lynching and supports racial moderation in an *Atlantic Monthly* article, which prompts school officials to ask for his resignation.

1902: **November 8** The National Education Association, the first teachers' union, is formed by the merger of The Chicago Teachers' Federation and the American Federation of Labor.

1903: **January 12** Industrialist John D. Rockefeller funnels his educational philanthropy through the newly chartered General Education Board.

1903: **April 18** Booker T. Washington's racial-accommodation approach to social and educational matters is publicly denounced by W.E.B. Du Bois with the publication of his book *The Souls of Black Folk*.

1903: **October 19** Judge William Gary of Augusta, Georgia, publicly declares that education makes black workers "unfit for the walks of life open to [them]," drawing national attention.

1904: **July 1** In a speech at the annual meeting of the National Education Association, labor leader Margaret Haley urges teachers to organize.

1904: **August 22** University of California President Benjamin Wheeler discourages women students from using a college education to do more than prepare them for marriage and motherhood.

1904: **October** In Florida, Mary McLeod Bethune founds the Daytona Literary and Industrial Institute for the Training of Negro Girls.

1905: **February 27** Seventy percent of male high school teachers and 53 percent of female high school teachers are college graduates, according to a report by Edwin Dexter to the National Society for the Scientific Study of Education.

1905: **April 16** Steel tycoon Andrew Carnegie endows the Carnegie Foundation for the Advancement of Teaching with $10 million.

1905: **July** One hundred percent of district superintendents and 94 percent of all high school principals are men, according to a National Education Association study of public school educators in cities.

1906: **April** Vocational skills are highlighted as important to teach to students in the state's public schools by the Massachusetts Commission on Industrial and Technological Education.

1906: **June** John Hope becomes the first African-American president of Morehouse College (then named Atlanta Baptist College), a historically black college.

1907: **March 12** Alain Locke becomes the first African American to receive a Rhodes Scholarship. No other African American scholar will be so honored for half a century.

1907: **October 16** In Hattiesburg, Mississippi, school officials ask the city council to create a separate school for the children of immigrants.

1908: **February 29** The Anna T. Jeanes Foundation is created with the goal of improving schools for black students in the rural South.

1908: **November 9** The U.S. Supreme Court upholds a Kentucky law prohibiting racial integration in private schools in *Berea College* v. *Kentucky.*

1908: **December** Seventy-two percent of New York City schoolchildren are either immigrants or the children of immigrants, according to a study by the U. S. Immigration Commission.

1909: **February 22** The annual meeting of the National Society for the Scientific Study of Education focuses on the subject of sex education.

1909: **July 29** In Chicago, Ella Flagg Young becomes the first female superintendent of an urban school system.

1909: **September** A part-time school for employed children and youth is created by the Cincinnati public school system as the nation's first continuation school.

1909: **November 18** New York City public schools ban football.

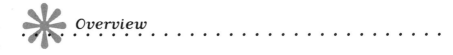

Overview

The American educational system faced many challenges during the earliest years of the twentieth century. The average American child attended only a few years of formal schooling, in which only the most basic grammar and mathematical skills were taught. More than two-thirds of American schools were located in rural districts. Most of these schoolhouses were one-room buildings staffed by teachers with little formal training. Classrooms were filled with students who generally ranged in age from five to twenty years old. The most common teaching methods were memorization and repetition. Unlike those in rural schools, urban students were grouped according to age and had a longer school year. Although children had been educated under these conditions for decades, many enlightened citizens began to realize that traditional schools were not serving their students well. They increasingly demanded that American education be reformed.

One of the primary concerns of many Americans was that society was changing rapidly during the 1900s and the nation's schools were failing to prepare their students for the many new challenges that lay ahead. The most important cultural shift was the economy's transformation. Large industrial corporations were gradually replacing agriculture and small manufacturing, which had once been the most powerful sectors of the economy. A related cultural shift was the increasing percentage of the population residing in cities, as rural Americans moved to urban centers in search of employment. They were joined in the cities' factories by millions of immigrants (many from southern and eastern Europe) who were arriving on America's shores. The working and lower classes were filled with native-born Americans who had little education and immigrants who often could not speak English. The nation's political and educational leaders realized that they must work to improve education in the Unites States to assist the millions of citizens who were unable to read, calculate numbers, or understand American history and social customs.

As American schools restructured to accommodate new circumstances, many educational leaders patterned their efforts after the examples set by successful businesses. Just as a CEO (corporate executive officer) leads a company, in the same way a superintendent would head a school system. Principals were seen as filling management positions, while teachers were akin to individual workers. More emphasis was placed on improving productivity and efficiency within each school. The connections between America's educational and economic institutions were strengthened, as employers became increasingly concerned about the ability of poorly educated employees to meet the demands of the changing workplace. In addition, vocational schools were founded across the nation to train students to enter industrial jobs upon graduation.

In 1900, 78 percent of all American children between the ages of five and seventeen were enrolled in schools; by 1910, that percentage had increased only slightly, to 79 percent. The amount of time the average student spent in school was much less than it is for students today. For example, in 1905, the average school year was only 151 days long and the average student attended school for only 105 of those days. Educators worked to increase the amount of time children would be required to spend in class. They also created programs to help students with special needs, such as the many foreign-born students who could not speak or understand English. Not only did these children learn the common American language, but they also were given special instruction on American social customs so that they would better conform to mainstream society. One of the most important reasons for the vast improvement of many schools was the higher quality of teachers entering the classroom. Many universities expanded their teacher education programs. It was no longer acceptable to hire teachers who were barely more educated than their students.

The movement to improve American educational standards gained steam throughout the first decade of the twentieth century. One of the movement's leading principles was that a formal education must meet not only the intellectual needs of students, but also larger social concerns. Many traditional teaching methods that were no longer useful were discarded and replaced by practices that stressed child development. Despite the push to improve the nation's educational standards during the early 1900s, very few students advanced beyond grade school. In 1900, only 11 percent of all children between ages fourteen and seventeen were enrolled in high school, and even fewer graduated. Those figures had improved only slightly by 1910. At the decade's end, the average number of school years completed by Americans over the age of twenty-five was only slightly more than eight.

Charles William Eliot (1834–1926) During his forty years as president of Harvard University, Charles William Eliot introduced innovative techniques that were adopted by other universities around the country. Eliot's principal innovation was the "elective system," which eliminated the traditional college practice of mandating a set curriculum for all students and gave students a greater role in determining their own education. He also shaped the development of the nation's secondary and elementary schools through his frequent writings, speeches, and involvement in educational reform panels. *Photograph courtesy of the Library of Congress.*

Margaret A. Haley (1861–1939) Margaret A. Haley headed the Chicago Teachers' Federation (CTF), the most militant teachers' organization in the United States. She fought tirelessly for better working conditions and pay for Chicago's elementary school teachers. Haley discovered that many of the shortages in Chicago's education budget were due to tax evasion by many of Chicago's largest corporations. Her efforts led to a court ruling that forced the corporations to pay their taxes, which provided more money for school improvements and teacher salaries.

John Hope (1868–1936) Born to a wealthy Scottish immigrant father and an African American mother, educator John Hope had blond hair, blue eyes, and a fair complexion. Despite his appearance, Hope identified himself as black. After a successful teaching career, Hope was chosen president of Morehouse College in 1906, the first black man to hold the position. Within months of his appointment, Hope faced a crisis as race riots gripped Atlanta. His firm leadership encouraged black students to return to campus. Hope was a strong voice for political and social equality for black Americans. He is considered one of the century's greatest advocates of black intellectual excellence. *Photograph reproduced by permission of Atlanta University Center—Robert W. Woodruff Library.*

Edward Lee Thorndike (1874–1949) Psychologist Edward Lee Thorndike advocated the application of scientific theories and techniques to a wide range of educational problems. He applied the results of animal experiments to human psychology by stating that students learn best when rewarded for correct responses. In 1909, Thorndike created a rating scale for tests measuring reading comprehension, geography, composition, arithmetic, spelling, and reasoning. Public school administrators and teachers began applying Thorndike's vision of learning theory, testing, and school efficiency in their schools by measuring and quantifying students' achievements. *Photograph courtesy of the Library of Congress.*

❖ THE CRUSADE FOR "AMERICANIZATION"

One of the greatest social issues of the 1900s was the impact of millions of new immigrants on American culture. Many native-born Americans were concerned that these "foreigners" did not share America's history and social traditions. The schools were viewed as the logical site where immigrant children could be exposed to America's customs and standards of dress and behavior. The theory was that the schools would help to assimilate, or absorb, the new immigrants into the United States's social and political mainstream. "Education will solve every problem of our national life, even that of assimilating our foreign element," stated one New York City high school principal in 1902.

The "Americanization Movement" was started in the 1890s by such patriotic organizations as the Daughters of the American Revolution (DAR), which believed that it was their duty to teach "American" values to immigrants. A related group, the Sons of the American Revolution (SAR), spent much of its annual income on programs that would demonstrate American traditions to the nation's newest citizens. Their efforts were even supported by the federal government. The U.S. Department of Commerce and Labor supplied funds to the SAR to print and distribute a pamphlet that (in fifteen different languages) announced the virtues associated with being a patriotic American.

In schools, the Americanization Movement provided instructors with classroom materials that stressed American history and heroes like George Washington, Benjamin Franklin, and Abraham Lincoln. One of the most frequently taught lessons was the need to obey the law. Students were also instructed in other methods that would more quickly allow them to remove any sign of their "foreignness." Immigrant boys and girls were told to speak English, dress in an American style, and always conform to American social customs. There was also concern that immigrant children were coming to schools without the proper means to care for themselves. Instructions were given on how to improve academically and on health tips, such as which foods to eat. The desire to Americanize students was so extreme that, in some cases, teachers would change their students' names to make them more "American sounding." For example, "Carlos" sometimes became "Charles" and "Maria" became "Mary." The main goals of the Americanization Movement were to provide new immigrants with the skills they needed to act like Americans and to eliminate any signs of cultural difference that might cause them to become isolated from the mainstream population. Students were taught how to read and speak in English, to fill out forms, and various other skills. It was hoped that they would, in turn, provide their parents with this much-needed information.

❖ NEW METHODS IN TEACHING

In the earliest years of the twentieth century, educators concentrated on determining the manner in which children learn and the subjects that are most important in shaping their intellectual and social skills. There were many disagreements among scholars on how best to teach American children. Educators generally fell into two opposing camps. "Traditionalists" believed that the mind, just like the body, is strengthened by frequent exercise. They stressed that mental activities were vital to develop a keen intellect, so they encouraged classroom teachers to emphasize frequent drills, memorization exercises, recitation, and strong academic discipline. An intellectually vigorous student was thought to be stimulated by such difficult subjects as Latin, Greek, and mathematics. Traditionalists resisted any change to the standard school curriculum that they felt would distract students from the core areas of study. The Traditionalists were opposed by the "Progressives," who believed that each individual

Between 1865 and 1915, about 25 million immigrants came to the United States. Most entered the country at Ellis Island in New York City. Courtesy of the Library of Congress.

Although kindergarten classes were relatively rare between 1900 and 1909, many educators thought that younger children were the best candidates for the Americanization process. Their minds were easier to shape than those of older children who had grown up accustomed to foreign traditions. In 1907, one early supporter of using kindergartens as centers of Americanization, Bruce James, said that in a child's earliest years a student can "breathe in the American spirit" through classroom "songs and flag drills [and] by its elementary practices." In 1909, the founders of the National Kindergarten Association (NKA) announced their belief that all public school systems should organize kindergarten programs to promote the ideals of assimilation.

child learns differently. One of the leading Progressive educators, Granville Stanley Hall (1844–1924), maintained that too much uniformity in schools hurt the child's naturally spontaneous impulses. Hall went onto say that humans progress through various stages of development and that one of the most significant stage is adolescence, the period between childhood and adulthood. Adolescents, he believed, were being educated incorrectly by the Traditionalist curriculum of rote memorization and repetitive drills. Hall and his fellow Progressives had three main beliefs about the nature of education. Above all, they strongly valued the scientific method as a basis for a good education. Secondly, they believed that strong educational institutions were the best tools for improving society. And finally, they believed that educators should focus mainly on students' individual needs. Although Traditionalist educators dominated the period from 1900 to 1909, the Progressives' ideals became increasingly more dominant over the next fifty years.

One of the nation's leading Progressive educators was Jane Addams (1860–1935), who was a pivotal force in America's settlement house movement. The settlement house movement, which began in England, was a loosely organized group of individuals and institutions that attempted to ease the harsh conditions endured by the poor in the late nineteenth century. Settlement workers stated that it was the moral duty of a society's educated members to close the gap between the rich and poor. They

Prep Schools

Although there were relatively few college preparatory schools during the early 1900s, those that did exist were most influential. Located primarily in the northeastern United States, "prep" schools, such as Exeter, Groton, and Hotchkiss, were highly regarded as fine educational institutions. Prep schools instructed students from some of the nation's most distinguished families. Many of the century's leading political figures were prep school graduates. Most of these schools were established between 1880 and 1910, and all were boarding schools for boys only. Prep schools were designed to mold a student's intellect and moral character to fully prepare him to face the challenges of college. These schools were financed by donations from wealthy philanthropists and catered to the cultural elite. High tuition costs made it impossible for boys of the middle and lower classes to attend these schools. Between 1900 and 1909, the average American adult worker earned $600 per year; most families thus could not afford to send their sons to study at these exclusive schools.

demonstrated their commitment to this ideal by living among the urban the poor, many of whom worked in factories. Their residence (or "settlement") in the neighborhood was to be a center of education. The best-known settlement in the United States was Addams' Hull House, located in Chicago. There, the neighborhood's immigrants and poor could participate in a variety of programs such as summer schools, concerts, and clubs designed to improve their lives. Children at Hull House were encouraged to be creative in their educational pursuits. Traditionalist demands for a set curriculum were set aside in favor of finding ways to connect the students' studies to their family lives. Furthermore, the Progressive idea of emphasizing the arts was a main feature of a Hull House education, as children were exposed to courses in music, drama, dance, poetry, and art appreciation. Not only was Hull House committed to improving the neighborhood through work in the classroom, but Addams and her supporters also fought for social justice as they demanded better pay for industrial workers and other improvements. The members of Hull House achieved many of their goals, which included clean and safer streets, improvements in health care, more parks and playgrounds for local children, and better working conditions.

Ethnic Differences in High School Entrances: Providence, Rhode Island, 1900

Ethnic Group	Percent Entering High School
Native whites, native parentage	36
Native whites, Irish parentage	11
Native whites, other parentage	23
Blacks	12
Irish	18
English, Scots, Welsh	8
All other immigrants	13
Total, all groups	18

Vocational education was another major Progressive idea that gained prominence during the decade. Progressives felt that a good education not only filled students with knowledge, but also provided them with a means to succeed within society. Many schools began to advocate the need for vocational education, which prepares students to become members of the workforce. In earlier decades, youngsters often learned vocational skills from family members or by serving as an apprentice to a craftsman. Schools now began to offer this training in order to produce laborers who could function better in the changing economy. Due to the strong emphasis on vocationalism during this era, many schools were referred to as "factories." By 1910, vocational programs were operating in twenty-nine states.

Students were often separated into different educational tracks while in school. On one track were the supposedly more intellectual students, who would follow a traditional academic curriculum. The other track consisted of students who were taught an industrial skill. Tests were used to determine on which track a student belonged. Although these tests were supposed to be "scientific," they frequently were used to remove the poor and racial or ethnic minorities from the academic track.

❖ COLLEGE LIFE

During the nineteenth century, the academic requirements for graduating from college were quite low. Students spent much of their time socializing and applying little effort to their studies. However, between 1865 and

The Rise of Business Schools

Many businessmen of the nineteenth century did not believe a college degree was necessary to achieve success in the financial world. Steel magnate Andrew Carnegie wrote in 1902 that those interested in careers in business should avoid college because the curriculum "injured" their minds. However, attitudes began to change during the 1900s as business-minded individuals recognized higher education could be an important asset. Slowly, schools of business were established at colleges throughout the nation. In 1908, Harvard opened its Graduate School of Business Administration after noticing that many of its undergraduates were choosing careers in business. By 1910, two-thirds of America's 150,000 undergraduates were enrolled in courses geared toward careers in business, like engineering or accounting.

1910 leading educators attempted to raise university standards through more intense academic requirements, which demanded strong scholastic achievement. Still, the first decade of the twentieth century is not remembered for its excellence in higher education. Fewer than one hundred American colleges and universities were considered to be academically challenging.

A university education was almost exclusively limited to white males from the upper classes. Nevertheless, women and minorities did make some inroads in higher education during the decade. Women made up 35 percent of college undergraduates in 1900 and 39 percent by 1910. In some institutions, female students endured discriminatory practices, as many educators believed that women were not suited to higher learning. Benjamin Wheeler, the president of the University of California, expressed a common attitude when he told his female students, "You are not like men and must recognize the fact.... You may have the same studies as the men, but you must put them to different use." Women, said Wheeler, were at the university "for the preparation of marriage and motherhood." At some colleges, female students were required to stand at attention until all their male counterparts were seated.

African Americans also encountered numerous restrictions in their efforts to receive a college education. Segregation laws limited blacks' opportunities for social, economic, and educational advancement. However,

Four women gather in a science laboratory at Wellesley College in Wellesley, Massachusetts, in the 1900s. Women made up 35 percent of the college undergraduates in 1900.

some African Americans did attain college degrees, often at historically black institutions. The leading African American scholars of the era were Booker T. Washington (1856–1915) and W.E.B. Du Bois (1868–1963). They had differing viewpoints on African-American higher education, but agreed that education was crucial to the ultimate success of black Americans.

Born a slave, Booker T. Washington was the most prominent African American at the turn of the century. Upon being freed from slavery after the Civil War, Washington attended a newly opened school for blacks in West Virginia. He later attended the Hampton Institute, a training school for blacks. He eventually took a position at the Tuskegee Institute, a black

ANNUAL SALARY RANGES OF PUBLIC SCHOOL TEACHERS IN SELECTED SOUTHERN STATES (1890–1910)

Alabama

Black teachers	$255-$311
White teachers	$215-$790

Florida

Black teachers	$319-$412
White teachers	$342-$676

Louisiana

Black teachers	$243-$340
White teachers	$418-$940

North Carolina

Black teachers	$204-$268
White teachers	$207-$506
National Average	$724-$1,102

college, in Alabama. Washington made headlines when, in an 1895 speech in Atlanta, he advocated that blacks and whites should attempt to support each other for the betterment of all. However, he did not support the idea of integration. Instead, he advocated the controversial position that blacks must stop demanding racial equality. He also stressed that whites must work toward ending discriminatory practices. His "Atlanta Compromise," in which he seemed to be trading social equality for economic opportunity, angered many blacks. Washington claimed it was better for most African Americans to learn a trade or an employable skill rather than acquire a "book education." Under his leadership, the Tuskegee Institute stressed industrial and vocational education over traditional academics.

The leading opponent to Washington's view was Du Bois, a brilliant scholar who graduated from Fisk University and Harvard, where he was the first African American to earn a doctorate. In 1903, he published *The Souls of Black Folk,* a series of personal and historical essays. In an essay titled "Of Mr. Booker T. Washington and Others," he attacked Washington's accommodating attitude toward segregation. He was certain Washington had harmed the cause of black equality by not advocating the necessity for African Americans to enter higher education. Du Bois believed that the African American community should strive to educate the "Talented Tenth," that portion of their race who possessed the ability to advance in academics. In his essay "The Talented Tenth" (1903), he wrote: "The Negro race, like all races, is going to be saved by exceptional men. The problem of education, then, among Negroes must first of all deal with the Talented Tenth, it is the problem of developing the Best of this race that they may guide the Mass away from the contamination and death of the Worst, in their own and other races."

❖ SOUTHERN EDUCATION

Between 1900 and 1909, many education reformers demanded better schools throughout America, especially in the South, where academic standards were particularly poor. The most significant problem facing

Students seated in a classroom at Tuskegee Institute, in Tuskegee, Alabama, in 1902. **Courtesy of the Library of Congress.**

reformers in the South was racial segregation. The educational opportunities available to black and white students were very different. The races attended separate schools and never mixed either academically or socially. Southern schooling was unequal, as the best schools, teachers, textbooks, and equipment were reserved for white students. African Americans had little political power and therefore could not employ political means to demand equal treatment for their children. Ironically, Progressive educators who journeyed South to improve educational standards often caused more harm than good to black Southerners, as their efforts primarily benefited the white schools. The Southern Education Board, which was created to improve the schools of all southern children, limited its aid to black schools due to pressure from white politicians.

A group of schoolchildren stand outside a one-room schoolhouse in Pinehurst, South Carolina, in the 1900s. Courtesy of the Library of Congress.

Another significant hurdle to improving southern education in the 1900s was that many poor whites (called "Plain Folk") believed the public schools were not necessary to the lives of their children. The Plain Folk claimed a formal education did little to prepare a child to face the hardships of everyday life. They felt the primary goal of education was simply to teach children how to live and work, and such instruction could be done informally, out of the classroom. The belief that education was a "waste of time" caused many southern parents to send their children to school only infrequently. It was not until after World War II (1939–45), when laws were passed by state legislatures compelling school attendance, that these attitudes began to change.

Some improvements in southern education were achieved during the decade. The most significant, perhaps, was the hiring of better-trained elementary and secondary school teachers. Northern philanthropists funded the education of many new teachers in the South. They believed that a better educated populace (which possessed solid reading and mathematical skills) was necessary for the development of a strong labor force and vibrant national economy.

For More Information

BOOKS

Fisher, Max W. *American History Simulations*. Huntington Beach, CA: Teacher Created Materials, 1993.

Greene, Laura Ofenhartz. *Our Century: 1900–1910*. Milwaukee, WI: Gareth Stevens, 1993.

Hakim, Joy. *An Age of Extremes*. New York: Oxford University Press, 1993.

Hall, Donald. *Lucy's Christmas* San Diego, CA: Browndeer Press 1994.

Hall, Donald. *Lucy's Summer*. San Diego, CA: Browndeer Press, 1995.

Kent, Deborah. *Jane Addams and Hull House*. Chicago: Children's Press, 1992.

Kittredge, Mary. *Jane Addams*. New York: Chelsea House, 1989.

Lee. George. *Interesting People: Black American History Makers*. New York: McFarland, 1989.

Peavy, Linda, and Ursula Smith. *Women Who Changed Things*. New York: Macmillan, 1985.

Pendergraft, Patricia. *Hear the Wind Blow*. New York: Philomel, 1988.

Rubel, David. *Scholastic Timelines: The United States in the 20th Century*. New York: Scholastic, 1995.

Ryan, Concetta Doti. *Learning Through Literature: School Studies*. Huntington Beach, CA: Teacher Created Materials, 1994.

Schroder, Alan. *Booker T. Washington: Educator and Racial Spokesman.* New York: Chelsea House, 1992.

Schwartz, Alvin. *When I Grew Up Long Ago.* New York: J. B. Lippincott, 1978.

Sloan, Carolyn. *Helen Keller.* New York: Chelsea House, 1987.

Stafford, Mark. *W.E.B. Du Bois: Scholar and Activist.* New York: Chelsea House, 1989.

WEB SITES

Education Reforms and Students at Risk: Historical Overview—Student Diversity. http://www.ed.gov/pubs/EdReformStudies/EdReforms/chap1a.html (accessed on August 8, 2002).

History of Indian Education in the United States. http://www.aiefprograms.org/ history_facts/history.html (accessed on August 8, 2002).

chapter four *Government, Politics, and Law*

1900: March 24 The Carnegie Steel Corporation is incorporated and becomes the nation's largest corporation.

1900: April 30 Under an act of Congress, Hawaii becomes a territory of the United States. It joins Arizona, New Mexico, Oklahoma, and Alaska as American territories.

1900: November 6 Republican presidential candidate William McKinley and his running mate, Theodore Roosevelt, defeat Democrat William Jennings Bryan.

1901: March 3 U.S. Steel is incorporated and is hailed as the nation's first billion-dollar corporation.

1901: September 6 President McKinley is shot by anarchist Leon Czolgosz while attending the Pan-American Exhibition in Buffalo, New York. Theodore Roosevelt becomes the twenty-sixth president of the United States.

1902: May 12 Pennsylvania's anthracite coal miners strike when mine owners reject their calls for a wage increase and an eight-hour workday. The strike continues until October and drastically limits the nation's coal supply.

1902: June 17 Congress enacts the Newlands Reclamation Act, which allows for the construction of irrigation dams throughout the West.

1902: July 1 Congress recognizes the Philippines as an unincorporated American territory; its citizens are given limited protections under the U.S. Constitution.

1903: January 5 The Supreme Court, in *Lone Wolf* v. *Hitchcock,* rules that Congress shall have total control over Indian lands; this decision violates earlier treaties.

1903: April 27 The Supreme Court upholds a clause in the Alabama constitution that effectively prohibits African Americans from voting.

1903: May 23 Wisconsin becomes the first state to hold direct primary elections.

1904: April 22 The Panama Canal officially comes under the control of the U.S. government.

1904: September 21 A woman is arrested for smoking publicly in New York City.

1904: October 19 The American Tobacco Company is formed by the merger of the Consolidated Tobacco Company and American & Continental Tobacco.

1904: November 8 Theodore Roosevelt is elected president of the United States. Republican majorities in both houses of Congress are increased.

1905: June 27 The Industrial Workers of the World (IWW) is organized by a combination of miners, socialists, and anarchists who are dedicated to overthrowing the capitalist system.

1905: **July 9** The "Niagara Movement" is established at Niagara Falls, Canada, where a group of black leaders (including W.E.B. Du Bois) advocate full civil and political rights for African Americans.

1905: **August 9-September 5** President Roosevelt works with Japan and Russia to seek a negotiated solution to the war they have been waging since February 1904. Roosevelt is awarded the Nobel Peace Prize for his efforts.

1906: **March 17** President Roosevelt coins the term "muckrakers" to define journalists who point out only the faults of large corporations without commenting on their positive social benefits.

1906: **June 30** Congress passes the Meat Inspection Act and the Pure Food and Drug Act.

1906: **September 22** Whites riot in Atlanta after hearing rumors of black men attacking white women. Twenty-one people are killed and the city is placed under martial law.

1906: **November 9-26** President Roosevelt is the first president to journey outside the United States when he travels to Panama to inspect the canal project.

1907: **January 26** Congress forbids corporations from making contributions to election campaigns of national candidates.

1907: **March 14** President Roosevelt bars Japanese immigration into the United States. His authority to do so stems from the recently passed Immigration Act.

1907: **November 16** Oklahoma becomes the forty-sixth state to join the union.

1908: **February 20** The Illinois Supreme Court holds that picketing is illegal.

1908: **May 28** The Child Labor Law for the District of Columbia, which prohibits the labor of children, is passed by Congress.

1908: **November 3** Republican William Howard Taft is elected the twenty-seventh president of the United States.

1909: **July 12** Congress proposes the Sixteenth Amendment to the U.S. Constitution, which authorizes a federal income tax. It is not ratified by the states until 1913.

1909: **September** Workers at the Triangle Shirtwaist Company in New York City are fired for attempting to form a union.

1909: **September 27** President Taft continues Roosevelt's land conservation policies as he prohibits drilling on three million acres of oil-rich land.

✳ *Overview*

American society was rapidly transforming at the dawn of the new century. The country as a whole was moving away from a rural agriculture-based lifestyle to an urban industrial economy. During the years 1900 to 1909, over eight million immigrants poured into the United States in search of jobs and opportunity. Less than fifty years before the turn of the century, five out of six Americans lived on a farm. By 1910, almost 50 percent of Americans resided in cities. These great cultural shifts provided the nation with many economic and political challenges throughout the 1900s.

As the nation became increasingly industrialized, the economy came under greater control of large corporations, which were overseen by a relatively few powerful executives. For example, by 1906 seven men controlled 85 percent of America's railroads. The federal government of this era favored a "laissez-faire" ("hands-off") economic policy that stated business should not be overly regulated by the state. Beginning in the late nineteenth century, corporations started to organize "trusts," or holding companies. Trusts were formed by businesses joining together to acquire stock and ultimately control their entire sector of the economy. Among the period's strongest trusts were those in the oil, gas, railroad, and meatpacking industries. Since they were largely free of government interference, trusts often treated their workers poorly, demanding that they labor for long hours at meager wages.

The push for reforming both the economic and political spheres grew during the 1900s, as citizens from all walks of life—farmers, factory workers, businessmen, settlement house workers, populists, socialists, and anarchists—began to demand changes in the manner in which the nation was operated. There were many calls to end government corruption at the local, state, and federal levels. Major American corporations were also targets for the reformers, who publicly complained about poor working conditions and child labor. More than five hundred thousand Americans were injured on the job each year and thirty thousand died in unsafe factories and mines. The workers' dissatisfaction was spread throughout the nation by "muckraking" journalists (reporters who wrote colorful stories about problems in the world of business), who saw it as their duty to expose the harsh treatment of American labor at the hands of corporate leaders. The government responded to these investigations by enacting numerous laws guaranteeing better treatment of employees and increasing product safety to protect the public. It was not only journalists who exposed the plight of industrial laborers, but also unions such as the Industrial Workers of the World (IWW), which organized to demand better treatment from their employers. Strikes became more common, and violence often erupted as business leaders and government officials sent in troops to forcefully end work stoppages. The clashes between labor and management were fierce, as labor grew more radical due to the influences of socialist members who saw the capitalist system as corrupt. (Socialists believed that workers should control all elements of the workplace and that every worker should benefit equally.)

The Supreme Court was slow to interfere in labor disputes at first. Gradually, however, the Court began to exert its power by reexamining the idea of interstate commerce. Throughout the decade the Court struggled with how to resolve the demands of business, which wanted to remain free of regulation to ensure economic progress, and labor, which sought to relieve the exploitation of the working class.

In many ways, America was a divided nation during the 1900s. Workers felt used and unappreciated by corporate executives. Immigrants often did not find the United States to be welcoming of their traditional customs, and they were told they must conform to the "American Way." The races were segregated in almost all respects. Blacks and whites did not attend the same schools or churches, and they rarely had any meaningful contact with one another. Many concerned citizens were aware of America's problems and were determined to reform much of the society. They worked to improve the nation's economic, political, and social ills.

The most significant political force of the century's first decade was President Theodore Roosevelt, who entered the White House in 1901 following the assassination of President William McKinley. During the late nineteenth century, the American presidency was a relatively weak office occupied by a number of bland politicians. Roosevelt was a dynamic figure who captured the nation's imagination with his vigorous physical presence and reforming spirit. He thrust himself into national and international issues and expanded American influence around the world. One of Roosevelt's most important policies was advocacy of environmental issues. As industry exploited America's land for its coal, iron ore, timber, and other raw materials, Roosevelt and fellow conservationists recognized that the environment was not abundantly plentiful and that the nation must protect its natural resources.

Charles Evans Hughes (1862–1948) After earning a law degree in 1884, Charles Evans Hughes began his public career in 1905 when he investigated the natural gas industries in New York. He next investigated the state's insurance industry, which was accused of misusing its clients' funds. Hughes's success as a reformer allowed him to win election as New York's governor. He served two terms, from 1906 to 1910, which were marked by widespread reforms throughout the state government. In 1910, President William Taft appointed him to the Supreme Court. Hughes resigned in 1916 to run for the presidency but was narrowly defeated by Woodrow Wilson. In 1930, President Herbert Hoover appointed him Chief Justice of the Supreme Court. He retired in 1941. *Photograph reproduced by permission of Archive Photos, Inc.*

Frances (Alice) Kellor (1873–1952) Upon earning a law degree in 1897, Frances (Alice) Kellor devoted her life to improving the conditions faced by women, minorities, and, the poor in American society. She advocated reforms in the judicial and penal systems, using modern sociological theories. Her first book, *Experimental Sociology, Descriptive and Analytical: Delinquents* (1902), is seen as a landmark text for its use of statistics in analyzing social problems. The book influenced generations of later scholars. Among those who sought her assistance in easing social problems were Theodore Roosevelt and Charles Evans Hughes. Under her leadership New York's banks began to be regulated, the slums were improved, and services to immigrants were expanded. *Photograph courtesy of the Library of Congress.*

Robert La Follette (1855–1925) Born into poverty, Robert La Follette rose from humble circumstances to earn a law degree in 1879. He was elected to Congress as a Republican representative from Wisconsin, in 1884. His politics began to change when he recognized that Wisconsin's political and corporate leaders seemed to be united to "cheat" the common people. In 1900 he was elected Wisconsin's governor. La Follette's time in office was marked by many reforms. His efforts served as an example to Progressives throughout the nation. To broaden his political ideals, he founded a national magazine in 1909, which was later called the *Progressive*. La Follette continued spreading his progressive ideas in the U.S. Senate, where he served until his death. *Photograph courtesy of the Library of Congress.*

Theodore Roosevelt (1858–1919) Born a sickly child to a wealthy New York family, Theodore Roosevelt was determined to overcome his weaknesses. He conditioned his body through vigorous exercise, and he improved his mind through many hours of study. Late in the century Roosevelt became involved in New York politics, serving as a civil service commissioner and, eventually, as a police commissioner. In 1898, he resigned as assistant secretary of the Navy to command the "Rough Riders," a volunteer cavalry in Cuba during the Spanish-American War (1898). His war-hero status allowed him to be elected New York governor. Roosevelt became vice president when McKinley won the presidential election and became president upon McKinley's assassination in 1901. Roosevelt focused on reforming corporate power and conserving America's national resources. *Photograph courtesy of the Library of Congress.*

William Taft (1857–1930) Ohio native William Taft was a lawyer long involved in Republican politics. In 1890, President Benjamin Harrison named Taft U.S. solicitor general. He became a federal judge in 1892, and in 1900 President William McKinley appointed Taft president of the Philippines Commission. He returned to the United States in 1904 to become Secretary of War under President Theodore Roosevelt, who counted Taft as one of his most trusted advisors. Taft won the presidency in 1908, but found the position unsatisfying. Increased tensions with former President Roosevelt led to a split within the Republican Party, which allowed Democrat Woodrow Wilson to win the White House in 1912. In 1921, President Warren G. Harding appointed Taft Chief Justice of the Supreme Court. He is the only American to serve as both a president and a Supreme Court justice. *Photograph courtesy of the Library of Congress.*

Booker T. Washington (1856–1915) Born into slavery, Booker T. Washington became the most influential African American leader and educator of the decade. Following emancipation (the freeing of slaves at the end of the Civil War), he worked in a salt furnace, in coalmines, and as a janitor to earn funds for his education. In 1881, the Tuskegee Institute, a Negro school in Alabama, was founded with Washington serving as its first principal. Washington was instrumental in developing the school into one of the nation's most prominent sites for educating African Americans. The most famous expression of his views was his "Atlanta Compromise" speech of 1895, in which he accepted racial segregation. *Photograph reproduced by permission of Schomberg Center for Research in Black Culture, New York Public Library.*

◆◆ *Topics in the News* •

❖ AMERICAN DOMESTIC POLICY: THE RISE OF REFORM

Giant corporations came to have a huge influence over government in the 1900s, as many American industries were consolidated into enormous trusts that dominated the national economy. The most significant corporate consolidation took place on January 1, 1901, when Andrew Carnegie (1835–1919) agreed to sell his steel company to J. Pierpont Morgan (1837–1913) for $480 million. Carnegie's operation was combined with Morgan's other steel properties to form U.S. Steel, the first American company to be capitalized at more than $1 billion. Among the other major industries consolidated during the decade were aluminum, life insurance, whiskey, sugar, lead, tobacco, coal, plate glass, wire nails, and smelting. Business leaders, most notably Morgan, saw consolidation as beneficial to the marketplace because it eliminated wasteful competition and gave corporate leaders more control over their employees.

While corporate titans like Morgan, Carnegie, and John D. Rockefeller (1839–1937) might have seen the trusts as positive economic tools, many Americans began to fear that the nation's business leaders were gaining too much control over the system. The nation witnessed the tremendous power of corporate America during a disputed merger of three railroads: the Northern Pacific; the Great Northern; and the Chicago, Burlington, and Quincy lines. To resolve the issue of who would control these railroad lines in the northwest part of the country, their corporate leaders formed a monopoly called the Northern Securities Company. Politicians soon discovered that by coming out against large corporations they could gain the public's confidence and win their votes. In 1900, the Republican presidential platform stated the party's opposition to "all conspiracies and combinations intended to restrict business, to create monopolies, to limit production, or to control prices." Once Republican Theodore Roosevelt entered the White House, he increased the government's efforts to limit corporations. In 1903, he proposed the creation of the Department of Commerce and Labor, which would directly focus upon and investigate corporate abuses. Congress also established a special fund, through which $500,000 would be budgeted to bring lawsuits against illegal business trusts.

Roosevelt, who earned his nickname "The Trust Buster," was quite successful in his campaign to limit corporations. His administration obtained twenty-four indictments against the trusts. The Supreme Court also handed down several notable anti-trust decisions during the early

Consumer Protection and *The Jungle*

In 1905, author Upton Sinclair (1878–1968) wrote *The Jungle*, a fictionalized account of the practices in Chicago's meatpacking industry. He exposed the awful conditions faced by stockyard workers as they labored in filthy packinghouses that often produced tainted meat products. The public was stunned and horrified by what Sinclair had described. Soon, calls came from across the country demanding that politicians do something immediately to protect America's food supply. In 1906, Congress passed the Meat Inspection Act and the Pure Food and Drug Act, which made it unlawful to mislabel or tamper with food and drugs distributed through interstate commerce.

twentieth century. In 1905, the court forbade the beef trust from trying to limit competition. In 1911, the court dissolved the Standard Oil Company, which once controlled 90 percent of the oil business. Another 1911 court order declared the American Tobacco Company an unlawful trust that would have to be disbanded. The Court decided many of its business-related cases by a formula that came to be known as the "rule of reason," which held that only "unreasonable" combinations in restraint of trade could be prohibited.

One of the most important areas of the government's reform efforts was rail transportation. Railroad owners, however, did not resist regulation but actually encouraged it. Railroad lines had been subject to varying rules in the different states in which they operated. The railroad owners also were often forced to pay kickbacks (payments for special favors) to the other trusts for the "privilege" of carrying their goods. The railroads turned to the federal government, which assisted them by passing the Elkins Act of 1903, which made the use of kickbacks an illegal act. In 1906, the government acted again to remedy the railroads' problems by passing the Hepburn Act, which strengthened the Interstate Commerce Commission (ICC) by giving it the power to reduce unreasonably high freight shipment rates.

The growing reform movement was not limited to concerns about the national government. Measures were passed in cities and states across America in an attempt to halt widespread corruption problems that

JUSTICE AND TERM

John Marshall Harlan, 1877–1911

Horace Gray, 1881–1902

Oliver Wendell Holmes Jr., 1902–1932

Melville Weston Fuller, 1888–1910

David Josiah Brewer, 1890–1910

Henry Billings Brown, 1890–1906

William Henry Moody, 1906–1910

George Shiras Jr., 1892–1903

William Rufus Day, 1903–1922

Edward Douglas White, 1894–1921

Rufus Wheeler Peckham, 1895–1909

Horace Hurton Lurton, 1909–1914

Joseph McKenna, 1898–1925

plagued many local communities. No state or city seemed to be spared from dishonest politicians who misused their governmental powers to line their own pockets or protect their criminal associates. The most corrupt politicians were active in New York City's Tammany Hall, a political machine (an organized group with political goals) that demanded special favors from politicians its members placed in office. It was common practice for local elected officials to sell their municipalities' gas, water, sewer, electricity, and streetcar rights to private companies (often headed by their friends). Even the police routinely took kickbacks and bribes from saloon and brothel owners to ignore their illegal activities. The victims of this widespread corruption were hardworking citizens, who were forced to pay astronomical utility rates, send their children to crumbling schools, walk unpaved and filthy streets, and drink contaminated water. The average people were at the mercy of those with powerful connections who knew they were safe from honest governmental intervention.

Urban political machines were powered by bosses who provided needed services to the many poor and immigrant families that populated

The Trials of Harry Thaw

One of the most notorious legal cases of the 1900s centered on the unstable character of Harry Thaw (1871–1947), the wealthy son of a Pittsburgh railroad magnate. On June 25, 1906, Thaw shot the famed architect Stanford White (1853–1906) three times with a pistol in the crowded rooftop restaurant of Madison Square Garden, which White had designed. Upon his arrest, Thaw claimed he killed White over an affair the architect was having with his wife, Evelyn Nesbit Thaw (1884–1966). Headlines across the nation described Thaw's history of emotional problems and the scandalous affair between his wife and White, which apparently pushed him over the edge. At his 1907 trial, the defense centered on Mrs. Thaw's story of her seduction by White and its disastrous effects on her husband's mind.

On April 12, 1907, the jury declared it was hopelessly deadlocked. At Thaw's second trial, in 1908, a jury found Thaw not guilty by reason of insanity. Soon afterward, Evelyn filed for an annulment (dissolution of marriage). Thaw's legal troubles continued when, in 1913, he escaped from a mental asylum. He was captured and declared sane in 1914. His final years were marked by frequent criminal behavior that included kidnapping, beating women, and whipping boys.

their neighborhoods. In exchange for feeding hungry families, providing jobs, posting bail for delinquent children, and providing hams and turkeys at the holidays, the machine demanded that those who received its assistance would vote for their chosen candidates on election day. Reformers recognized the urgency in throwing corrupt politicians out of city hall. In 1902, Lincoln Steffens (1866–1936) published an article titled "The Shame of the Cities" in *McClure's* magazine. His story, which revealed the corrupt practices commonplace in local governments, was so powerful that citizens throughout the nation organized into groups demanding reforms. A number of measures were eventually instituted to take control away from the corrupt officials and place it into the hands of public servants who were truly dedicated to good government. Some of the most successful reforms included election of stronger mayors, election of council representatives from the city at large instead of from individual districts, creation of city managers, and establishment of juvenile courts.

❖ THE CRUSADE FOR CONSERVATION

The rise of the Industrial Revolution during the nineteenth century concerned citizens who recognized that many of America's idyllic natural landscapes were being destroyed in the name of big business. At the turn of the century, the timber industry, the nation's second largest, was still rapidly expanding. The frontier was disappearing as forests were cut down, mines were excavated, and grazing lands were fenced off. It was becoming increasingly difficult for America's natural resources to meet the heightened demands of its people. Although politicians had been attempting to promote conservation since the 1890s, it was not until Theodore Roosevelt became president that the federal government placed great emphasis on preserving the environment and its natural resources.

Roosevelt was a native of New York, but spent much of his life exploring the West. His love of the outdoors spurred his fight to preserve a portion of the nation's wilderness. The president believed it was his duty to inform his fellow citizens of the need for conservation. He expressed his ideas in speeches and writings. In 1905, Roosevelt urged Congress to create the U.S. Forest Service to maintain the national forests. This was followed a year later by the Antiquities (or National Monuments) Act of 1906, which allowed the president to set aside chosen areas based upon their scientific or historic importance. Although many of his plans to preserve the environment succeeded, Roosevelt was not without strong opposition. Western farmers, ranchers, lumberjacks, and miners disliked the government's interference in their businesses. They criticized the Forest Service and its power to limit their activities within the designated 200,000,000 acres of National Forests. The western industrial interests soon convinced their congressional representatives to block a number of the president's environmental protection proposals.

❖ THE BULLY PULPIT

The modern presidency began in the late nineteenth century, when William McKinley (1843–1901) expanded the chief executive's powers during the Spanish-American War (1898; a war between the United States and Spain over distant territorial possessions). Unlike earlier "caretaker" presidents, McKinley actively involved himself in legislation and took on other responsibilities. Following McKinley's assassination in 1901, President Theodore Roosevelt at first followed his predecessor's example and later exceeded it. Roosevelt believed the president should exert his political power and influence to the greatest extent. Soon after assuming office, he stated his intent to become involved personally in numerous matters, including regulating trusts, strengthening the military, advocating conserva-

OPPOSITE PAGE
President Theodore Roosevelt (left) and environmentalist John Muir stand on Glacier Point, in the Yosemite Valley, California. Roosevelt loved the outdoors and did much to conserve the nations' national resources.
Reproduced by permission of the Corbis Corporation.

The Assassination of William McKinley

On September 6, 1901, President William McKinley arrived at a reception at the Pan-American Exposition in Buffalo, New York. Three Secret Service agents, four special agents, and several soldiers protected him. As the president stood in a reception line to greet members of the public, a young man with a bandaged hand approached him. The man, whose name was Leon Czolgosz, shot McKinley twice with a revolver. Emergency surgery was performed on the president, but he succumbed to his wounds and died a week later, on September 14. Czolgosz went to trial only nine days after the president's death. He was an anarchist whose hatred of social injustice caused him to view all leaders as enemies of the people. Furthermore, he advocated violence as a proper means for changing the social structure. Czolgosz refused to take the stand, was found guilty, and was electrocuted on October 29. His terrible actions thrust the young, progressive Vice President Theodore Roosevelt into the Oval Office. When told of McKinley's death, conservative Republican Senator Mark Hanna said, "Now that damned cowboy is president." Roosevelt would soon distinguish himself as one of the greatest presidents of the century.

tion, and regulating labor. He referred to the presidency as a "bully pulpit" where he could publicize issues that demanded the public's attention and persuade legislators to accept his agenda. The Roosevelt administration was also known for its fairness in political appointments. Whereas other administrations often used appointments to fulfill personal or political obligations, Roosevelt appointed candidates to high posts based on their merit.

President Roosevelt was extremely popular with the general public. A charismatic man, he was highly intelligent and also displayed a love of sports and the outdoors. Voters responded to his strong, rugged personality. However, conservative members of his Republican Party were not pleased with his independent nature or his left-leaning positions. Roosevelt understood the nation was entering an era of change. He worked to develop political and social reforms that were more favorable to the common citizens rather than the social elite and Republican Party leaders. In 1904, Roosevelt faced weak Democratic opposition and was easily elected to another term as president. He won a majority of the popular vote in thirty-three of the forty-five U.S. states, and he won 336 electoral votes,

OPPOSITE PAGE
A lynching victim hangs from a tree. **Courtesy of the Library of Congress.**

the highest total ever. Roosevelt pledged that he would not seek another term as president. His chosen political heir was William Howard Taft of Ohio, who was the president's friend and secretary of war. With Roosevelt's assistance, Taft easily won the White House in 1908.

❖ RACIAL VIOLENCE AND ETHNIC DISCRIMINATION

A great racial divide marked American society of the 1900s. The repression faced by African Americans was most graphically demonstrated by the numerous lynchings that occurred throughout the nation. Mobs of whites frequently administered their own form of violent justice against blacks by torturing them and hanging them for public display. Lynching was not restricted only to the rural South but also was practiced in many states in other parts of the country. Between 1895 and 1905, there were more lynchings in the United States than there were legal executions. Unlawful mobs often claimed they were punishing rapists and protecting the honor of white women. Those who committed this violence on blacks were seldom arrested or prosecuted, since few witnesses would ever come forward to testify against them.

One of the worst incidents of racial violence occurred in Streetsboro, Georgia, in 1904. Two blacks, accused of killing a white family, were dragged from a courtroom and burned alive by an angry mob. Many Americans were horrified by these events and demanded changes in the legal system. It would not be until later in the century that African Americans received their full constitutional rights and lynching became a federal offense.

Blacks were not the only population to be mistreated by the white majority. Asian immigrants were seen as a "yellow peril" that threat-

Jim Crow

By the 1900s most of the South was completely segregated as white politicians drafted a number of laws that effectively denied blacks their civil rights. In *Plessy* v. *Ferguson* (1896), the Supreme Court approved the creation of "separate but equal" racial societies. Beginning in 1900, the "separate but equal" rule was applied to nearly every aspect of southern society. Movie theaters, water fountains, hotels, restaurants, swimming pools, and other public accommodations were declared "off limits" to blacks. These restrictions, known as "Jim Crow" laws, effectively relegated African Americans to an inferior social status.

ened white laborers. Congress and the Roosevelt administration enacted laws limiting the numbers of Japanese and Chinese immigrants.

❖ AMERICAN FOREIGN POLICY

The United States increasingly demonstrated its influence in the world at the beginning of the twentieth century. America's involvement with foreign affairs expanded as the United States began to acquire territories in the Caribbean and the Pacific. In the first decade of the century, the United States, for the first time in its history, claimed possession of overseas territories. Following the Spanish-American War in 1898, the United States took possession of Guam, Wake Island, and the Philippines. Puerto Rico was also acquired, and Hawaii was annexed by the United States during this period. Americans were divided over whether the nation should retain control of these lands and the extent to which it should be involved with the territories' internal affairs. Business leaders saw these lands as new, untapped markets for their commercial goods, while reformers and missionaries saw the inhabitants of the territories as "primitives" in need of salvation and guidance from the white man.

America's chief rival in the Pacific was Japan, which had become more modern and westernized during the nineteenth century. In 1904, a war erupted between Japan and Russia over disputed lands in northern China. President Roosevelt and many Americans strongly supported the Japanese, but remained concerned that a prolonged international conflict might develop into more widespread warfare that threatened trade. Roosevelt directly involved himself in the war in 1905 when he hosted a peace conference to resolve the dispute. The president's decision to insert himself forcefully into international affairs was based upon his realization that America could play an important role in maintaining the balance of world power. For his efforts to end the Russo-Japanese War, Roosevelt was awarded the Nobel Peace Prize in 1906. He was the first American to earn that high honor.

Theodore Roosevelt's international dealings were based on protecting America's political, geographic, strategic, and commercial interests. This approach led him to involve the United States with many foreign nations, including Great Britain, Italy, Canada, Cuba, and Germany. His diplomatic activities were backed by a strong American military, which was capable of enforcing the president's will. Roosevelt's policy came to be known as "big stick" diplomacy, which was named after one of his favorite African proverbs: "Speak softly and carry a big stick."

One of Roosevelt's most significant foreign plans involved the construction of a canal that would connect the Pacific and Atlantic Oceans. In 1903, the United States entered into an agreement with Colombia to construct a canal. In return for a ninety-nine-year lease on the Canal Zone, the U.S. proposed to pay Colombia $10 million and to make an annual payment of $250,000 beginning nine years after the treaty was ratified. Colom-

The Panama Canal under construction in 1890. The canal officially came under the control of the U.S. government in 1904. **Reproduced by permission of Archive Photos, Inc.**

bia's government rejected the treaty, however, and this resulted in Panama (the Colombian province where the canal was to be built) declaring itself an independent state. U.S. warships, which were ordered to assist the Panamanians, aided the revolt to ensure construction of the canal. Within days, the United States formally recognized the new nation of Panama. In 1906, Roosevelt became the first president to travel abroad when he toured the Canal Zone. Canal construction finally began in 1914.

❖ MAJOR LEGAL DECISIONS OF THE 1900S

Many important court cases were decided during the 1900s and would have great impact on American society throughout the century. One of the most significant was the Northern Securities Case. Here the Supreme Court ruled that a railroad monopoly was unlawful, since it restrained trade and the freedom of commerce. This verdict, in what was known as the Northern Securities Case, gave the government power in breaking up trusts that operated against the public's interests. Soon, President Roosevelt was moving against beef, oil, and tobacco trusts. In *Lochner* v. *New York* (1905), the Supreme Court decided a state had the right to regulate working hours or conditions only if it could prove that such regulations were fair and appropriate.

For More Information

BOOKS

Allen, Robert, and Michael Derman. *William Jennings Bryan: The Golden-Tongued Orator.* New York: Mott Media, 1992.

Blackwood, Gary. *Rough Riding Reformer: Theodore Roosevelt.* New York: Benchmark Books, 1998.

Brownlie, Alison. *Crime and Punishment: Changing Attitudes 1900–2000.* New York: Raintree, 1999.

Fradin, Judith Bloom, and Dennis Brindell Fradin. *Ida B. Wells: Mother of the Civil Rights Movement.* New York: Houghton Mifflin, 2000.

George, Charles. *Life Under the Jim Crow Laws.* New York: Lucent Books, 2000.

Grant. R.G. *Racism: Changing Attitudes 1900–2000.* New York: Raintree, 1999.

Havens, John. *Government and Politics (Life in America 100 Years Ago).* New York: Chelsea House, 1997.

Klingel, Cynthia, and Robert Noyed. *William McKinley: Our Twenty-Fifth President.* New York: Child's World, 2001.

MacDonald, Fiona. *Women in Peace and War: 1900–1945.* New York: Peter Bedrick Books, 2000.

Maupin, Melissa. *William Howard Taft: Our Twenty-Seventh President*. New York: Child's World, 2001.

McRae, Anne, ed. *Atlas of the Twentieth Century*. New York: Peter Bedrick Books, 2000.

Olson, Kay Melchisedech. *Chinese Immigrants, 1850–1900 (Coming to America)*. New York: Blue Earth Books, 2001.

Parks, Edd Winfield, and Gray Morrow. *Teddy Roosevelt: Young Rough Rider*. New York: Aladdin Paperbacks, 1989.

Patrick, John. *The Supreme Court of the United States: A Student Companion*. New York: Oxford University Press, 2001.

Pringel, Laurence. *The Environmental Movement: From Its Roots to the Challenges of a New Century*. New York: HarperCollins, 2000.

Roosevelt, Theodore; with Shelley Swanson Saterem, ed. *The Boyhood Diary of Theodore Roosevelt, 1869–1870: Early Travels of the Twenty-Sixth United States President*. New York: Blue Earth Books, 2000.

Stearman, Kay. *Women's Rights: Changing Attitudes 1900–2000*. New York: Raintree, 1999.

Wormser, Richard. *The Rise and Fall of Jim Crow: The African American Struggle Against Discrimination*. New York: Franklin Watts Inc. 1999.

WEB SITES

Alexandria Archaeology Museum—Discovering the Decades: 1900s. http://oha.ci.alexandria.va.us/archaeology/decades/ar-decades-1900.html (accessed on August 8, 2002).

1860–2000: General History. http://cdcga.org/HTMLs/decades/1900s.htm (accessed on August 8, 2002).

The 1900s: 1900–1909. http://archer2000.tripod.com/1900.html (accessed on August 8, 2002).

Story of Immigration in the U.S.: Ellis Island. http://brownvboard.org/brwnqurt/04-1/04-1a.htm (accessed on August 8, 2002).

White House Historical Association—Timeline. http://www.whitehousehistory.org/04_history/subs_timeline/a_presidents/frame_a_1900.html (accessed on August 8, 2002).

chapter five *Lifestyles and Social Trends*

1900: Some of the new automobile brands introduced to the public are Franklin, Peerless, Stearns, Packard, and Auburn.

1900: One in twelve American marriages ends in divorce.

1900: Cocaine is removed from the recipe for Coca-Cola.

1900: There are more than 1.3 million telephones in the United States.

1900: November 3-10 The nation's first auto show is held in Madison Square Garden. It is sponsored by the newly established Automobile Club of America.

1901: The Socialist Party of America is formed.

1901: King Camp Gillette manufactures the modern safety razor.

1901: The Boys' Corn Club and Girls' Home Club are founded. These organizations are the forerunners of the 4-H Club.

1901: January 22 Britain's Queen Victoria dies. Her son, Edward VII, succeeds her to the throne.

1901: October 16 President Roosevelt sparks controversy by inviting black leader Booker T. Washington to dine at the White House.

1902: Ragtime music sweeps the nation.

1902: March 4 The American Automobile Association (AAA) is established.

1902: June 15 A trip on the Central Railroad line from New York to Chicago takes twenty hours.

1903: *The Great Train Robbery,* directed by pioneer filmmaker Edwin S. Porter, is screened. It is regarded by many as the first Western film.

1903: The Ford Motor Company introduces its Model A automobile.

1903: It is reported that 93 percent of America's 2.3 million miles of roads are little more than dirt paths, unsuitable for automobiles.

1903: September 1 Massachusetts is the first state to issue automobile license plates.

1904: The first automobile road maps are published.

1904: Phonograph rolls are used for sound recording and become a popular entertainment.

1904: April 15 Andrew Carnegie donates $5 million to establish a fund honoring those who risk their lives to save others.

1904: June 15 More than 100,000 people, mostly immigrant women and children, are killed when a steamboat called *The General Slocum* burns in New York City's East River.

1904: October 27 The first completed segment of the New York City subway system is opened to the public.

1905: The Rotary Club is established in Chicago as a volunteer community service organization.

1905: Novocaine, a painkilling medicine, is introduced.

1905: The World's Fair is held in Portland, Oregon.

1905: The first nickelodeon begins operation in Pittsburgh, Pennsylvania.

1905: *The Clansman,* a controversial novel that glorifies the Ku Klux Klan, is published.

1906: Winsor McKay's popular comic strip *Little Nemo in Slumberland* is introduced to American newspapers.

1906: **August 14** Black soldiers riot in Brownsville, Texas, and are later dishonorably discharged from the military by President Roosevelt, despite little evidence of their guilt.

1906: **December 24** The first radio broadcast of words and music is made by Reginald Aubrey Fessenden in Massachusetts. Only those on fishing and military boats are able to hear his broadcast.

1907: Florenz Ziegfeld inaugurates his Follies on a New York stage.

1907: The soda pop Canada Dry Ginger Ale is introduced.

1907: Paris fashion designers spark international controversy by creating "short" skirts, which have hemlines ending just above a woman's boot.

1907: **September 12** The *Lusitania,* the world's largest steamship, completes its first voyage.

1908: The first skyscraper, which stands forty-seven stories (612 feet) tall, is completed in New York City.

1908: The electric iron and toaster are introduced by General Electric.

1908: Winsor McKay presents the first animated cartoon, *Gertie the Dinosaur.*

1908: **August 12** Ford introduces the Model T automobile, which is affordably priced at $850.

1908: **September 17** Thomas Selfridge becomes the first person to die from wounds suffered in a plane crash. Orville Wright, the plane's pilot, is also seriously injured in the crash.

1909: The Metropolitan Life Insurance Tower is completed in New York City. It remains the world's tallest building until 1913.

1909: The Alaska-Yuko-Pacific Exposition opens in Seattle, Washington.

1909: **March 7** Arbor Day, which celebrates nature, is first established in California in honor of famed botanist Luther Burbank.

1909: **August 2** The Indian-head penny, which had been in circulation for fifty years, is replaced by the Lincoln penny.

✳ *Overview*

The United States shed many of its nineteenth-century styles, traditions, and beliefs as it entered the modern era. America in 1900 was vastly different from the rural, farm-based economy populated largely by Anglo-Saxons of a hundred years before. The country was becoming increasingly urbanized, and its cities were filling with immigrants from nations around the world. Immigrants and their children accounted for the majority of the population in cities like Cleveland, Ohio; Chicago, Illinois; New York, New York; Pittsburgh, Pennsylvania; and St. Louis, Missouri. Many of these newly arrived Americans could neither read nor write English and, therefore, were able to undertake only manual labor and factory jobs.

Tensions between native-born Americans and others arose, especially when immigrants realized that America was not the idyllic land they had imagined. Schools struggled with educating immigrant children, who were unfamiliar with both the language and the American way of life. The business sector encountered its own struggles as labor unions fought to receive better wages and benefits from employers who were unaccustomed to negotiating with workers.

Women made many advances during the century's first decade, as they built upon the accomplishments of those who had demanded more equal treatment during the 1800s. In the 1900s, women were increasingly joining the workforce at all levels. Immigrant and working-class females began to be employed outside the home as opportunities in manufacturing and retailing expanded. Educated women made greater advances in both the academic and professional spheres as they joined the ranks of doctors, lawyers, and professors who had previously been all male. By 1910, nearly 40 percent of America's undergraduates were female. Women were also greatly involved in social work and religious causes.

Jane Addams inspired generations of women into action through her efforts at Hull House, a settlement house in Chicago that educated and helped immigrants. Many women, such as Carry Nation, joined the Temperance Movement (a movement to limit alcohol consumption) and rallied for the prohibition of alcohol. Another social concern that drew the attention of many women was suffrage, or the right to vote.

Other significant changes affected America's lifestyle and social trends. Technological inventions, such as the automobile and the airplane, improved transportation and made travel more available and affordable to the average citizen. Mass production of cars in the early 1900s brought the United States into the automobile age, which had a profound impact on the culture for decades. The motion picture industry was gradually being developed as well, and within the decade, America was captivated by this new mode of entertainment. Advances were also made in radio transmission. Furthermore, the American home became filled with such new appliances as the electric light, icebox, phonograph, telephone, and vacuum cleaner.

American styles and fashions also evolved, as Victorian formalism slowly gave way to more modern styles of dress, architecture, furniture, and interior design. Women, inspired by the popular magazine illustrations of the "Gibson Girl" as the representation of the new modern female, began to wear more fashionable clothes. The growth of department stores and national catalogues allowed styles to be regularized across the country. Frank Lloyd Wright revolutionized the field of architecture with his fluid use of space, natural light, and environmentally friendly designs. The Arts and Crafts movement spread from Europe to some sections of America during this period. Soon, many homes were showcasing fine, handcrafted furnishings and exotic styles. Although some Americans were reluctant to embrace modernism and its emphasis on all things new and contemporary, many others came to recognize the customs, styles, and tastes of the Victorian period as being totally outdated.

Jane Addams (1860–1935) In the late 1880s, Jane Addams visited Toynbee Hall, an early settlement house in Europe where she discovered a group of educated men and women living in an urban slum in order to assist their poor neighbors. Returning to her native Chicago, she established Hull House in 1889 as a similar place where artists and educators could settle to improve social conditions. Addams spent the rest of her life running Hull House and trying to further improve labor conditions, women's suffrage, and the peace movement. *Photograph courtesy of the Library of Congress.*

Evangeline Cory Booth (1865–1950) Evangeline Cory Booth was born the year her father began the East London Revival Society. The organization was later called the Christian Mission and subsequently known as the Salvation Army. Booth devoted her life to the Salvation Army. She would take the Army and its mission to help the poor and spread Christian principles throughout the world. Startled by the poverty she saw when she arrived in New York, she began bread lines and organized efforts to feed children. Booth became a powerful orator who championed the causes of women's rights and the drive toward prohibition. In 1934 she was elected general of the Salvation Army, a position she held until she retired in 1939. *Photograph reproduced by permission of the Corbis Corporation.*

W. E. B. Du Bois (1868–1963) W.E.B. Du Bois was one of the most influential African American thinkers of the twentieth century. Educated at Fisk and Harvard Universities, Du Bois strongly criticized Booker T. Washington's segregationist beliefs. He believed prejudice could be eliminated through sociological methods. He proposed that "The Talented Tenth" of the black population should receive a university education and lift up their peers with the knowledge they had gained. Active in the National Association for the Advancement of Colored People (NAACP) for decades, Du Bois spoke publicly on the need for free African nations and greater equality for blacks in the United States.

Mary Baker Eddy (1821–1910) Christian Science founder Mary Baker Eddy was a sickly child and frequently plagued by illness into adulthood. In 1866, she founded the Christian Science movement, which states that only the mind is real while the body and its frailties are merely illusions and can be cured through mental effort. She spread her message through *The Christian Science Journal* (now *The Christian Science Monitor*), starting in 1883. Eddy remained leader of the "Church of Christ, Science" from its incorporation in 1879 until her death in 1910.

Charlotte Perkins Gilman (1860–1935) After her marriage and the birth of her daughter in 1885, feminist writer Charlotte Perkins Gilman grew depressed and complained that she had lost her freedom. In 1887, she separated from her husband and began a career as a writer, advocating women's economic and sexual rights. "The Yellow Wallpaper," her horror story about a woman slipping into insanity, received much praise when it was published in 1892. Later Gilman was scorned for her decision to send her daughter to live with her former husband. After a long battle against cancer, she committed suicide in 1935. *Photograph reproduced by permission of the Corbis Corporation.*

Emma Goldman (1869–1940) Immigrant Emma Goldman embraced socialist and anarchist ideas, which advocated the overthrow of the capitalist system. She became a political revolutionary, criticizing much of modern American society. In 1892, Goldman was imprisoned for attempting to kill industrialist Henry Clay Frick. She said marriage must be abolished, as it enslaves women, and proclaimed women must be sexually free. Goldman spread her ideas through her journal *Mother Earth,* which began publication in 1906. In 1917, she was jailed for interfering with the military draft. Deported in 1919, Goldman spent the remainder of her life in Europe. *Photograph courtesy of the Library of Congress.*

Carry Nation (1846–1911) Carry Nation remains the twentieth century's greatest opponent of alcoholic beverages. Her hatred of liquor grew from her first husband's death from alcoholism. She launched a national crusade against alcohol. She began by holding prayer vigils in saloons, but when that proved ineffective she became more radical in her methods. Beginning in the 1890s, she attacked several taverns with rocks, bricks, and her infamous hatchet. Nation was often arrested following her efforts, and she supported her cause financially by selling souvenir hatchets. She died in 1911, several months after being beaten by a female saloon owner.
Photograph courtesy of the Library of Congress.

Louis Comfort Tiffany (1848–1933) Louis Comfort Tiffany, the son of famed jeweler Charles Tiffany, was one of the nation's leading interior decorators. In 1883, he decorated several rooms in the White House. Tiffany believed that glass was an essential element in creating an elegant living space. In 1878, he formed the Tiffany Glass Company, which developed a technique where color could be added to glass without stain. The resulting pieces were known for their shimmering beauty. At the 1900 Paris Exposition, Tiffany was recognized as the master of the "art nouveau" style. *Photograph reproduced by permission of Archive Photos, Inc.*

◆◆ *Topics in the News* . . . .

❖ AN EVOLVING SOCIETY

For more than one hundred years, white men of northern European heritage dominated the social structure of the United States. They held all elective offices and major cultural posts and, therefore, shaped social policy from their singular perspective. The world around them, however, was changing, as women, minorities, and people from other cultural backgrounds became increasingly vocal in their desires to have American society reflect their own experiences.

The twentieth century opened with a great tide of immigrants arriving on the nation's shores. Between 1865 and 1915, approximately twenty-five million immigrants journeyed to America. This was more than four times the number that had come to the country during the fifty years before the Civil War (1861–65). Many of these arrivals entered the United States at Ellis Island in New York City, where they were processed, inspected, and checked for disease. Unlike the majority of the previous century's immigrant population, these people generally originated from southern and eastern Europe—Italy, Russia, Poland, Greece, and the Austro-Hungarian Empire. They spoke little or no English, often had minimal education, and lacked familiarity with American culture. Their reasons for coming were varied, but they all shared in the belief that America was the land of opportunity, where people could be free from political and religious persecution, own their own land, gain an education, and earn more than enough money.

Although the United States did offer them chances to better their lives, the newly arrived immigrants soon discovered America was not without its own hardships and struggles. Native-born Americans often felt as if "foreigners" were overrunning their country. Immigrants drew further mistrust from native-born Americans when they established insular neighborhoods. In these neighborhoods they could live and work while speaking their native languages, eating ethnic foods, and participating in their own traditions. Many Americans resented the immigrants' desire to live in the United States without fully abandoning their native customs. Isolated from much of the larger culture, many immigrants relied on their families, their churches, and ethnic organizations for support. Some native-born Americans feared that immigrants would accept lower wages, thereby taking away jobs from citizens. In reality, the jobs that the immigrants were able to secure were often the lowest paid, most physically intensive positions available. They toiled in mines, mills, factories, sweatshops, and on shipping docks.

The Birth of the NAACP

In 1909, a group of white and black reformers founded the NAACP (National Association for the Advancement of Colored People). The group's beginnings can be traced to the works of W.E.B. Du Bois and others of the Niagara Movement (a civil rights movement, started in 1904 and headed by Du Bois), who protested white America's mistreatment of blacks. The NAACP's goal was to use the legal system and the media to end racial injustice. While the majority of the group's members were black, wealthy whites largely financed its efforts. The group continued its struggle throughout the century.

The tensions encountered by immigrants to the United States were more than matched by those facing African Americans and other racial minorities during the first decade of the 1900s. A strict color line separated the races, and there were few chances for white and black cultures to make meaningful contact. The two most significant obstacles to racial unity were segregation and violence. Race riots and public lynchings, although on the decline from past decades, were still common occurrences. Between 1900 and 1914, there were approximately 1100 lynchings in the United States, with more than one hundred such incidents in 1900 alone.

A more subtle form of racial injustice was evident in the many instances of segregation throughout the country. Segregation, the separating of the races, became legally formalized in many parts of the United States during the 1890s and 1900s. Statutes called "Jim Crow" laws prohibited whites and blacks from sharing the same educational institutions, transportation, hotel accommodations, and entertainment facilities. In both the North and South, whites generally regarded blacks as inferiors who must be kept as far away as possible. Many southern states were particularly harsh in their treatment of African Americans, as they instituted poll taxes, grandfather clauses, and literacy tests to block them from their right to vote. It would not be until 1965 that many blacks again were able to vote without these barriers. The prejudice of many whites forced most blacks into lives of poverty, meager education, and menial jobs. Given these circumstances, many blacks left their homes in the rural Deep South in search of opportunity in cities like New York, Philadelphia, Baltimore,

Temperance and Prohibition

The temperance movement was one of the most vigorous social causes during the late nineteenth century and its advocates only grew stronger in the early 1900s. The movement blamed a majority of America's social ills upon the abuse of alcohol and therefore demanded that all liquor be banned from the United States. Temperance advocates denounced liquor, not only for damaging the mind and body of the drinker, but also for negatively affecting the drinker's work and family lives. Many of these reformers were women who gathered together to hold prayer vigils outside saloons. The two best-known temperance organizations were the Women's Christian Temperance Union (WCTU) and the Anti-Saloon League (ASL), both of which demanded the prohibition of the manufacture, sale, and consumption of alcohol. Although most of their demonstrations were peaceful, anti-liquor activist Carry Nation made headlines by attacking taverns with rocks, bricks, and a hatchet.

and Memphis. Unfortunately, racial discrimination was also widespread in these new surroundings. Blacks were not the only minorities to be mistreated early in the twentieth century, as Native Americans and Asian immigrants also endured prejudice from white people.

Another group challenging American culture was women, who had been largely excluded from participating in any organizations outside the home. A widely held belief supporting this exclusion was that women were morally superior to men. Early feminists tried to debunk this idea by announcing that they were concerned not only about "family issues" within the home, but also with the larger social ills. Increasingly, women joined together to form their own labor organizations and activist groups, such as the Women's Christian Temperance Union, the National Congress of Mothers, and the National Association of Colored Women. They strove to improve social welfare programs, join trade unions, and earn suffrage, or the right to vote. In 1909, a massive strike by members of the International Ladies' Garment Workers Union (ILGWU) demonstrated that working-class and immigrant women could unite to improve conditions in the workplace. However, in the struggle for suffrage, female activists were not as successful. By 1913, only eight sparsely populated western states had given women the right to vote.

The Settlement House Movement

The settlement house movement exemplified much of the era's reforming spirit. Social activists worked to overcome problems caused by poverty, disease, and lack of education. They settled within the slum communities that dominated many of the nation's cities. The idea was that a reformer could understand the lower classes' problems only by experiencing their harsh conditions for themselves. A number of settlement houses were founded around the turn of the century. They included the Henry Street Settlement in New York City, James Reynolds's New York University Settlement, and Hull House in Chicago, which was established by Jane Addams. Like Addams, many settlement workers were women, usually in their twenties and thirties, who possessed a fervor to promote the Christian values of equality and mutual responsibility. At the settlement houses people were educated in academic, cultural, and practical knowledge. Classes were taught on sewing, cooking, reading, music, and art appreciation, and on how to conform to middle-class standards of behavior and cleanliness.

Children were another social group who faced many challenges during the decade. The late nineteenth and early twentieth centuries were marked by the exploitation of millions of children who received little or no formal education because they needed to work to help support their families. It was commonplace to see young boys and girls toiling in coalmines, textile mills, factories, sweatshops, and on farms throughout the United States. Regulations to improve or limit child labor were implemented during the decade largely due to the efforts of Lewis Hine (1874–1940), a photographer who exhibited stark pictures of grimy, exhausted young workers from across the country. In 1908, the National Child Labor Committee (NCLC) passed the first child labor law. However, the problem of working children would not be solved in America for decades.

❖ RELIGION IN AMERICA

America's religious practices were becoming more diverse throughout the early 1900s. Protestantism, which had served as the nation's spiritual core since the American Revolution (1775–83), increasingly was confronted with immigrants who journeyed to the United States with their

A group of children stand in front of Hull House in Chicago, Illinois. The settlement house was founded by Jane Addams.
Reproduced by permission of AP/Wide World Photos.

own faiths. During the century's first decade, Roman Catholicism, Eastern Orthodoxy, Judaism, and some Asian religions saw their American memberships quintuple. Those in sectarian movements such as The Church of the Latter-Day Saints (Mormons), Christian Science, Seventh-Day Adventists, and Jehovah's" Witnesses also attracted more converts.

"Millennialism," the religious belief concerned with the "end days," when God will supposedly begin a thousand-year reign of peace on Earth, divided many Protestants during the decade. Pre-millennial believers maintained that the second coming of Jesus Christ would be preceded by a time when social conditions worsen. Once Jesus returns, however, the pre-millennialists believed, his arrival would eliminate all human social problems. Post-millennialists, on the other hand, believed that human

Church Membership at the Turn of the Century

In 1900, the U.S. population was approximately seventy-six million with almost one-third (twenty-six million) of Americans belonging to an organized church. The membership numbers of the top eight denominations were:

Roman Catholics	8,000,000
Methodists	5,500,000
Baptists	4,000,000
Presbyterians	1,500,000
Lutherans	1,000,000
Disciples of Christ	1,000,000
Episcopalians	600,000
Congregationalists	600,000

attempts to perfect society will bring about the "millennium," and that Jesus will return only after humans have created the kingdom of heaven on Earth. The liberals and social reformers who made up the majority of the post-millennialists said the kingdom of God came through human, not divine, intervention in society. They spread their beliefs not only through preaching, but also through their efforts to improve social ills.

Another point of religious discussion centered on "Social Christianity," the belief that religious ideals must be tied more strongly into the capitalist system. Many Social Christians were politically socialist and preached the need for an economic system based upon Christian love. The legacy of connecting religion more strongly to modern social problems led many to call for better treatment of workers, the abolition of child labor, a six-day work week, and arbitration in labor disputes. Social Christianity led to the founding of several important social agencies, such as settlement houses, Young Men's and Women's Christian Associations (YMCA, YWCA), and crusades like the temperance movement.

❖ ADVANCES IN TRANSPORTATION

American transportation made tremendous advances in the early 1900s due largely to technological innovations that made it easier and

A woman drops money into a Salvation Army kettle on the streets of New York City in 1906. The Salvation Army is a Christian social service organization. Reproduced by permission of the Corbis Corporation.

more affordable for average citizens to move from place to place. The electric streetcar allowed urban centers to expand, as it became possible for people to commute from their downtown workplaces to new suburban neighborhoods. Los Angeles's rapid growth would have been impossible without the streetcar. For example, a streetcar company founded in 1901, called Pacific Electric, was transporting more than 250,000 Los Angeles riders over more than 1000 miles of track each day by 1920.

While the electric streetcar was a marvel, its cultural significance was dwarfed by the rise of the automobile, which truly revolutionized America and the world throughout the twentieth century. American inventors had experimented with various "horseless carriages" since the 1880s, but these motorized vehicles were unreliable. The 1900s began with innovators like Freeman and Francis Stanley experimenting with a steam-driven car they called the "Stanley Steamer." Although it was a fast auto, the Steamer was able to hold only enough water for a twenty-mile journey. In Cleveland, Rollin H. White created the first touring car, which was also powered by steam. One of the more successful automobile pioneers was Ransom Olds, whose cars were sturdy, lightweight, and economical. The person most noted for advancing the auto industry in the 1900s was Henry Ford (1863–1947), who introduced the Model A, his first car, in 1903. He pioneered the development of assembly-line production methods to reduce his manufacturing costs, pricing his autos at $850 each so that the average consumer could afford to buy one.

As cars became increasingly commonplace, Americans were more able to travel greater distances from their homes. Driving was seen to be a pastime that demanded its own set of unique fashions. Since most cars were open to the elements, passengers wore long canvas-like coats called "dusters" to protect themselves from poor weather and the dust from dirt roads. Soon drivers and passengers became irritated by the terrible conditions of America's roads. "Good Roads" campaigns were instituted across the country demanding that cement or asphalt be spread to ease travelers' comfort.

❖ A FASHIONABLE ERA

For most Americans at the beginning of the century, clothes were important not for their fashion, but for their utility. Most women made clothes for themselves and their families by following standard patterns available from companies like McCall's and Butterick. Most immigrant and working-class families struggled merely to survive, so people were not concerned with adopting the latest styles. A person from these classes might have only one set of formal clothes that was generally worn for church services or special occasions.

The wealthy, however, could afford to stay current with the latest fashion trends from London or Paris. Women from the United States's leading families, such as the Astors, the Vanderbilts, and the Roosevelts, adopted

*Camille Clifford, the
original "Gibson Girl."*
**Reproduced by permission of
the Corbis Corporation.**

Illustrator Charles Dana Gibson (1867–1944) was, perhaps, the American who most strongly influenced female fashion from the 1890s until World War I. In numerous magazine illustrations he depicted tall, elegant girls with soft, luxurious hair piled upon their heads. The "Gibson Girl," as this persona came to be known, symbolized a new, vital type of American woman who was stylish, high-spirited, and independent. Many women took to wearing the "Gibson Girl" look not only because they admired its fashion, but also because it indicated that the wearer was a new breed of woman less bound by strict social customs. The era's most famous "Gibson Girl" was Alice Roosevelt (1884–1981), the teenaged daughter of the president, who shocked high society by speaking her mind, partying late into the night, and defying almost all social conventions.

current European styles and, in turn, influenced the look of middle-class women. The dominant look adopted by these women was noted for its ultrafeminine style, which highlighted the female form in an S-shaped silhouette. This silhouette style started with a bell-shaped skirt covering stiff taffeta petticoats. A small bustle with a train of fabric was added, as was a linen corset with whalebone stays that flattened the stomach and created the illusion of a tight, wasplike waist while also exaggerating the wearer's bust and hips. A stiff collar caused the women to hold their heads up. These clothes, although popular, were extremely uncomfortable, because they caused the woman's body to tilt forward awkwardly. Finally, stylish hats trimmed with lace, ribbons, feathers, stuffed birds, and buckles completed the outfit. Hats became so lavish that in 1905, for example, the Sears, Roebuck catalog offered more than seventy-five different kinds of ostrich feathers for women's hats. As the decade progressed, women's hats grew increasingly big and were often worn with a face veil.

Middle- and working-class women could not afford the expensive styles favored by the elite. However, women of more modest means did favor an important fashion innovation: the shirtwaist, a blouse designed to be worn with a long skirt. It was a popular garment since it was ideal for active working women. The shirtwaist became so popular that by 1905 the Sears, Roebuck catalog offered more than 150 variations, which ranged in price from 39 cents to $6.95. The shirtwaist was most important in that it came to rep-

The Price of Fashion—Prices at the Pegues, Wright Department Store, Junction City, Kansas; 1909

LADIES' WEAR:

Tailor-made suit	$10
Skirt	$4
Shoes	$1.50
Silk petticoats	$5

MEN'S WEAR:

Fancy suit	$9
Trousers	$1.25
Hat	$2
Coat and vest	$7
Work shoes	$1.25

resent the era's new breed of working woman. These "pink-collar" workers were usually employed in corporate offices as secretaries, stenographers, and typists. Pink-collar workers earned approximately ten dollars per week, double the income of their female peers in the factories. They also entered the popular culture as the glamorous heroines of serialized stories in romance magazines.

Wealthy men of the early 1900s favored apparel that was as stylized and formal as that worn by their female counterparts. An upper-class man of the 1900s generally wore a dark frock coat, a waistcoat (vest), and striped trousers at the office. He spent his leisure time wearing a lounge jacket with pointed lapels and narrow trousers with a crease down the center of the leg. Like women, men dressed formally for dinner. They also wore nearly as many accessories as the women did. Elite men favored silk top hats in winter and straw Panama hats in the summer. Other accessories included pocket watches that hung from long chains, leather gloves, white shirts with stiff, detachable collars, and umbrellas or walking sticks. The average working man wore a simplified version of the gentleman's wardrobe. One of the most significant stylistic changes of the period was the increased importance of the barbershop, which came to

Lifestyles and
Social Trends

TOPICS IN THE NEWS

*Typical apparel wore by
men in the 1900s.*
**Courtesy of the Library
of Congress.**

A Mail-Order House

In the early 1900s, entire houses could be purchased through a catalog. All the pieces arrived through the mail. Sears, Roebuck and Company began selling houses in its 1908 catalog. The store sold practically everything needed to construct a house: lumber, roofing, flooring, doors, windows, paint, heating, wiring, and plumbing. The buyer also received blueprints to follow in building the house himself. Sears claimed that one of its smaller models could be built in an average of 352 carpenter-hours. Between 1909 and 1934, Sears sold more than one hundred thousand houses. Although the program was ended in 1937, at the end of the twentieth century many of the mail-order homes remained standing and in good condition.

resemble a men's social club. Men could go there to smoke, drink, and tell stories not suited for a decent woman's ears.

❖ ARCHITECTURE AND INTERIOR DESIGN

During the nineteenth century, American architectural styles looked primarily to the past for inspiration. By the dawn of the 1900s, however, that attitude had begun to change, as artists and architects were increasingly inspired by the natural world. Louis Sullivan (1856–1924) and many other architects journeyed to Chicago to experiment with new styles in the years following the great 1871 fire that destroyed most of the city. Known as "the Chicago school of architecture," Sullivan and his followers stressed that buildings could be both useful and dignified, as they were constructed to be in harmony with their surroundings. This theory was summed up in Sullivan's famous phrase "form follows function." Their belief was that a more natural design style would lead to a truly American form of architecture. One of Sullivan's students, Frank Lloyd Wright (1867–1959), emerged during the 1900s to become one of the nation's leading architects. Wright developed the "Prairie Style" of design, which was characterized by horizontal lines, spacious interiors, and leaded glass windows. One of Wright's most discussed works of the era was the Frederick G. Robie House (1909) in Chicago, which successfully integrated elements from the natural environment into the home. Wright also transformed American interior design as he broke from Victorian traditions by creating houses with high ceilings, many windows, and innovative uses of light and space.

Another influential decorating style of the 1900s was the "Arts and Crafts Movement," which was marked by a rejection of the Victorian era's highly ornate furnishings. Leaders of the Arts and Crafts Movement, like Charles (1868–1957) and Henry (1870–1954) Greene, proclaimed that American homes should contain simpler, handcrafted furnishings. The Greenes were especially noted for helping to introduce the bungalow style, or smaller houses with open spaces and naturalistic colors, to the United States. In home furnishings, the 1900s became known for the designs of Gustav Stickley (1858–1942) who crafted simple, comfortable furniture that was more sturdy than the delicate, fragile pieces that exemplified the Victorian style.

For More Information

BOOKS

English, June. *Transportation: Automobiles to Zeppelins.* New York: Scholastic, 1995.

Greene, Carol. *John Phillip Sousa: The March King.* Chicago: Children's Press, 1992.

Greene, Janice. *Our Century: 1900–1910.* Milwaukee: Gareth Stevens, 1993.

Harvey, Brett. *Immigrant Girl: Becky of Eldridge Street.* New York: Holiday House, 1987.

Kalman, Bobbie. *Early City Life.* New York: Crabtree, 1994.

Kalman, Bobbie. *A One Room School.* New York: Crabtree, 1994.

Karl, Jean. *America Alive: A History.* New York: Philomel, 1994.

Kent, Deborah. *Jane Addams and Hull House.* Chicago: Children's Press, 1992.

Lawson, Don. *The United States in the Spanish-American War.* New York: Harper, 1976.

Littlefield, Holly. *Fire at the Triangle Factory.* Minneapolis: Carolrhoda, 1996.

Shea, George. *First Flight: The Story of Tom Tate and the Wright Brothers.* New York: Harper Collins, 1997.

Stewart, Gail. *1900s.* New York: Crestwood, 1990.

Wilson, Kate. *Earthquake! San Francisco, 1906.* Austin: Raintree, 1993.

WEB SITES

Alexandria Archaeology Museum—Discovering the Decades: 1900s. http://oha.ci. alexandria.va.us/archaeology/decades/ar-decades-1900.html (accessed on August 8, 2002).

1860–2000: General History. http://cdcga.org/HTMLs/decades/1900s.htm (accessed on August 8, 2002).

The 1900s: 1900–1909. http://archer2000.tripod.com/1900.html (accessed on August 8, 2002).

20th Century Fashion History: 1900s. http://www.costumegallery.com/1900.html #1900Ladies (accessed on August 8, 2002).

Medicine and Health

1900: The U.S. Army's Yellow Fever Commission identifies the mosquito as the carrier of the deadly disease.

1900: Trichinosis, a disease caused by a worm present in undercooked pork, is shown by Dr. George Blumer to be widespread throughout the nation.

1900: March 6 A Chinese laborer in San Francisco is discovered to have died of bubonic plague. More than one hundred people will die of the disease during the next four years.

1900: The first ceasarean section in Wyoming is performed by Dr. C. Dana Carter.

1901: Congress grants permanent status to the U.S. Army Nurse Corps.

1901: Dr. William Herbert Rollins presents research that X rays may be deadly.

1901: The Rockefeller Institute for Medical Research is established.

1902: Congress passes the Biologics Control Act to regulate vaccines and antibiotics.

1902: The McCormack Institute for Infectious Diseases is established in Chicago.

1902: A case of pellagra, an ailment caused by malnutrition, is diagnosed in a poor farmer. The disease will become more common throughout the decade, especially in the South.

1903: Dr. Arnold Schwyzer performs the first surgery to remove a foreign body from a lung.

1903: Dr. Frederick George Novy founds the first medical unit to fight rabies in the United States.

1903: Homer Folks conducts the first survey of tuberculosis in New York City.

1904: Dr. Hugh Hampton Young performs the first radical operation on a cancerous prostate gland.

1904: Dr. John LaRue founds People's Hospital, the first general hospital in Nevada.

1904: Dr. John Erlanger conducts important research on the kidneys.

1905: New Orleans suffers through the last yellow fever epidemic to hit the United States.

1905: Dr. Ludvig Hecktoen proves humans can transmit measles to one another.

1905: Dr. Louis Blanchard Wilson devises a fast, accurate laboratory analysis method for surgical tissue samples.

1905: The American Medical Association, the Association of American Medical Colleges, and the Southern Medical College Association form the Council on Medical Education to reform medical schools throughout the United States.

1906: A pathologist at the University of Chicago, Dr. Howard Taylor Ricketts, begins research that will later identify ticks as the cause of Rocky Mountain spotted fever.

1906: The Pure Food and Drug Act becomes law.

1906: The Meat Inspection Act is passed by Congress after widespread public concern over unsanitary conditions in the meatpacking industry.

1906: The first biochemical research facility in the nation is founded at Johns Hopkins Medical School in Maryland.

1906: Dr. James Hall Mason Knox Jr. organizes the Baby's Milk Fund in Baltimore, Maryland, to provide milk to infants in low-income families.

1907: Dr. James Ewing and others founds the American Association for Cancer Research.

1907: Dr. Simon Flexner and other researchers develop a serum treatment for epidemic spinal meningitis.

1907: Drs. C. C. Guthrie and F. H. Pike successfully experiment with using plasma to replace blood during surgery.

1907: The first successful tissue culture is performed using frog embryos.

1907: Bernarr MacFadden is arrested for mail distribution of obscene materials: a magazine issue explaining to men how venereal disease is contracted.

1908: Drs. E. Z. Hawkes and Edward Wharton Sprague perform the first blood transfusion.

1908: The Connecticut Society for Mental Hygiene, the world's first mental health organization, is established.

1908: The American Society for Clinical Investigation, the first organization devoted to patient research, is founded.

1909: The College of Medical Evangelists is founded in Loma Linda, California, by Seventh-Day Adventists.

1909: Dr. William Snow Miller develops a seminar on medical history that becomes a model for universities across the nation.

1909: The Committee of One Hundred on National Health recommends a federal health department.

1909: Philanthropist Nathan Straus founds the first tuberculosis prevention facility for children in New Jersey.

Overview

Medical care during the nineteenth century had been a curious mixture of science, home remedies, and quackery. Many of the most basic elements of modern medicine, such as sophisticated hospitals, physician education and certification, and extensive medical research did not exist. By the turn of the century, however, both public and private institutions were beginning to advocate practices designed to improve public health. Local governments initiated programs to clean their water supplies and control the disposal of human, animal, and industrial wastes, which are known to spread disease if not handled in a proper manner. Many of the nation's finest colleges and universities raised their standards for admittance into medical schools to ensure that only the most qualified students graduated as doctors. Also, vaccinations were increasingly employed as a means to stop many diseases that plagued Americans.

Although health care of the nineteenth century appears quite primitive when compared to modern medical practices, significant scientific advances were made during the period. One of the most important of these breakthroughs occurred in the 1840s, when it was discovered that inhaling ether, or chloroform gases, lessened the pain of surgery. Physicians were now able to perform longer and more complicated procedures on their sedated patients. Another medical breakthrough of the era was the work of Englishman Joseph Lister, who pioneered the use of antiseptics. Previously, it had been unheard of to perform operations and other medical procedures in a sterile environment. Doctors and nurses commonly treated their patients with filthy hands and instruments that spread infection and disease. Medical equipment also made great advances during the nineteenth century, as doctors were introduced to such new tools as the stethoscope, laryngoscope (a device used to view the larynx), improved microscopes, the medical thermometer, and the X ray. Drugs were better administered with the new hypodermic needles and anesthesia machines. Furthermore, there was an increase in laboratory research, as scientists began to research cellular, bacterial, and viral causes for disease, which led to the creation of more sophisticated drug remedies.

Medicine not only evolved in scientific knowledge, but also as a profession. For decades in America, one did not need any formal medical training to call oneself a doctor or to treat patients. Many Americans relied upon local practitioners, not trained physicians, for diagnosis and treatment. But in the early nineteenth century, even professional physicians were required to meet rigorous standards. To improve the medical profession's social standing, a group of concerned doctors organized the American Medical Association (AMA) in 1848. After the Civil War (1861–65), other similar organizations, along with medical journals, were established to spread knowledge and raise the qualifications for becoming a physician. One of the leaders of this movement was Harvard University president Charles Eliot. He and others sought to strengthen medical licensing laws and bolster medical education throughout the nation. Their efforts would greatly improve the quality of health care in the country. Soon women and minorities were being trained as doctors and nurses in significant numbers for the first time in American history.

The nineteenth century witnessed numerous improvements in American health and medicine, but many important problems lingered as a new century dawned in 1900. Among the most significant were the lack of hospitals, laboratories, and medical libraries throughout the country. In 1900, most surgeries were still performed in the home. Another area of concern was the flood of tonics, home remedies, and patent medicines produced and sold to many gullible Americans by charlatans and quacks promising miracle cures. Frequently these "medicines" were little more than alcohol and "snake-oil," which were completely ineffective and occasionally even dangerous.

The twentieth century opened with many Americans desiring to reform the problems that had plagued the nation's health care system for generations. The AMA, which had been a weak organization for decades, became stronger and aggressively pushed for reforms. Government and local campaigns were also organized to combat such diseases as yellow fever, pellagra, tuberculosis, and hookworm, which plagued many communities. American medicine of the 1900s slowly improved, as dedicated men and women worked toward improving the nation's health.

John J. Abel (1857–1938) John J. Abel is known as the "father of American pharmacology." At Johns Hopkins University, he spent nearly four decades establishing the methods by which pharmacology was to be taught and researched in the United States. Pharmacology is the branch of medicine concerned with the actions of drugs within the human body. Pharmacologists develop and test new drugs to understand their therapeutic or toxic effects on humans. Among Abel's most significant contributions to medicine was his demonstration that proved the presence of amino acids in the blood and his research into the possibility of creating an artificial kidney. *Photograph courtesy of the Library of Congress.*

William Crawford Gorgas (1854–1920) William Crawford Gorgas came from a prominent Alabama family and was encouraged to undertake a military career. When he failed to be admitted to West Point, Gorgas entered Bellevue Medical College. In 1880, he was appointed a surgeon in the Army Medical Corps. While stationed in Texas in 1883, he contracted yellow fever. Upon recovering from the deadly disease, his immunity led him to be stationed at other posts where yellow fever was commonplace. During the Spanish-American War, he served as head of sanitation in Havana, Cuba. While in Cuba, he destroyed many of the mosquito breeding grounds where yellow fever was concentrated. His success in Cuba led to international fame and, in 1904, Gorgas was named chief sanitary officer at the Panama Canal construction site. Within a year, yellow fever had been eliminated from the Canal Zone. *Photograph reproduced by permission of AP/Wide World Photos.*

Walter Reed (1851–1902) Walter Reed's research into the causes and transmission of tropical fevers made him one of the most respected physicians of the early twentieth century. One of his more important studies centered on typhoid fever. Chairperson of the typhoid commission in Cuba during the Spanish-American War, Reed demonstrated that filthy camp conditions were ideal breeding grounds for the flies that spread the disease. His greatest triumph, however, occurred when he headed the Yellow Fever Commission in Cuba in 1900. Reed's research showed the disease was spread by only one type of mosquito under unique conditions. A campaign to wipe out that mosquito was soon begun. By 1902, the campaign had succeeded, and yellow fever was eradicated throughout Cuba.

Photograph reproduced by permission of AP/Wide World Photos.

❖ DEVELOPMENTS IN THE MEDICAL PROFESSION

Numerous individuals of varying skills and qualifications practiced medicine in the 1900s. Although the American Medical Association (AMA) had been founded in 1848, it remained a weak organization for more than fifty years. Because few physicians attended the group's annual meetings, the AMA did not expand beyond its bases in the East and Midwest. Internal disagreements further hindered the group's efforts to address the major medical concerns of the era, such as the relatively poor quality of medical education, the rise of physician specialization, and competing health philosophies. By 1900, however, the AMA had begun an intense period of reform designed to enhance the organization's standing across the nation. A Special Committee on Reorganization was created to offer recommendations on improving the AMA. The committee advocated strengthening the AMA's ties to state and local medical societies. By the end of the decade, the AMA had achieved significant growth. The group, which had only 8,400 members in 1900, had grown to more than 70,000 by 1910. With its newly increased rolls, the AMA began to exert greater influence in public health issues. For example, the AMA vigorously supported the 1906 Pure Food and Drug Act and other pieces of legislation, and sought to limit the amount of patent medicine sold to the public. By the end of the decade, the AMA had grown into one of the nation's most influential professional associations. It was able to shape the American health system for decades. It began to take on responsibilities such as setting standards for medical practices, granting admission into the profession, reprimanding doctors for misbehavior, and advocating policies to ensure the public's health.

Health care in the 1900s was further enhanced by greater diversification in the membership of the American medical community. African Americans had a long history of participating in the medical profession before the beginning of the twentieth century. James Derham is widely regarded as the first black physician in American history. Born into slavery, Derham learned his medical skills from his owner, Dr. James Kearsley Jr., a prominent doctor. After being sold to Dr. Robert Dove of New Orleans at the end of the Revolutionary War (1776–83), Derham continued his studies and eventually developed a thriving practice. In 1837, James Smith became the first African American to earn a medical degree, which he received from the University of Glasgow in Scotland. A decade later David Smith became the first black person to graduate from an American medical school. In 1864, Rebecca Lee became the first black woman to earn a medical degree when she graduated from the New England Female Medical College (now the Boston University School of Medicine).

Despite such advances, relatively few blacks were able to enter the medical profession until after the conclusion of the Civil War, in 1865. Several medical schools dedicated to educating former slaves were founded around that time, the earliest being Howard University in Washington, D.C., in 1869. By the turn of the century, more than a dozen medical schools for blacks were operating in Louisiana, Tennessee, North Carolina, Kentucky, Maryland, and Pennsylvania. Only four of these institutions, which graduated a vast majority of the nation's black physicians prior to 1920, survived until 1910. Black doctors of the era kept informed on contemporary issues through their own professional organization, the National Medical Association, which continues to thrive.

Despite being restricted by segregation, blacks in medicine in the 1900s accomplished several major achievements. Black hospitals were

*An operation takes place
at a hospital in the early
1900s. Reproduced by
permission of the
Corbis Corporation.*

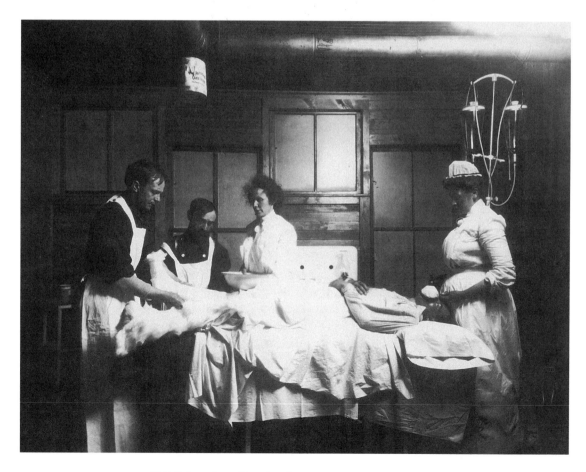

Dentist William Morton of Boston first demonstrated the use of anesthetics to sedate patients during surgery in 1846. For the next fifty years, surgical patients received anesthesia mainly from medical students or doctors with little training in the potentially lethal procedure. By the end of the century, nurse Alice Magaw was one of the first individuals to practice anesthesiology full-time. Magaw performed the procedure on more than fourteen hundred patients during her career, mostly for Drs. William W. and Charles H. Mayo (1861–1939). Between 1892 and 1906, she authored several important articles explaining anesthesia for doctors across the nation. A true pioneer for women in medicine, Magaw was so well respected that Dr. Charles Mayo proclaimed her the "mother of anesthesia."

opened to care for patients who had been refused treatment at white health-care facilities. Two of the most prominent of these black hospitals were the Lincoln Hospital in Durham, North Carolina, (founded in 1901) and Mercy Hospital in Philadelphia (founded in 1907). Among the most noteworthy African American physicians of the period included George C. Hall, Benjamin Covington, and Daniel H. Williams, who developed a means to suture (stitch) ruptured spleens in 1904. Black doctors of the era had few white patients, and black students were refused admittance to many established medical schools until after World War II (1914–18).

Like African Americans, women faced a difficult struggle to attain a medical education in the late nineteenth century and early twentieth century. Most Americans believed women were emotionally unfit to assume the role of doctor. Americans widely believed that women were too physically and intellectually weak to participate in any endeavor outside the domestic sphere. Still, some women were able to enter the field. In 1850, the Women's Medical College of Pennsylvania was established, and it graduated its first class of eight women the following year. By the 1890s, women could attend some of the same medical schools as their male counterparts. Some medical schools admitted women to their ranks only due to financial necessity. In 1890, for example, Johns Hopkins University was in dire straits and announced a unique plan to improve its economics: The school would accept women for medical education if wealthy female patrons would donate $500,000 to the university endowment. Other colleges followed the Johns Hopkins example and permitted the enrollment of female medical students. Female doctors comprised approximately 5 percent of the nation's physicians in 1900. Nearly seven thousand female

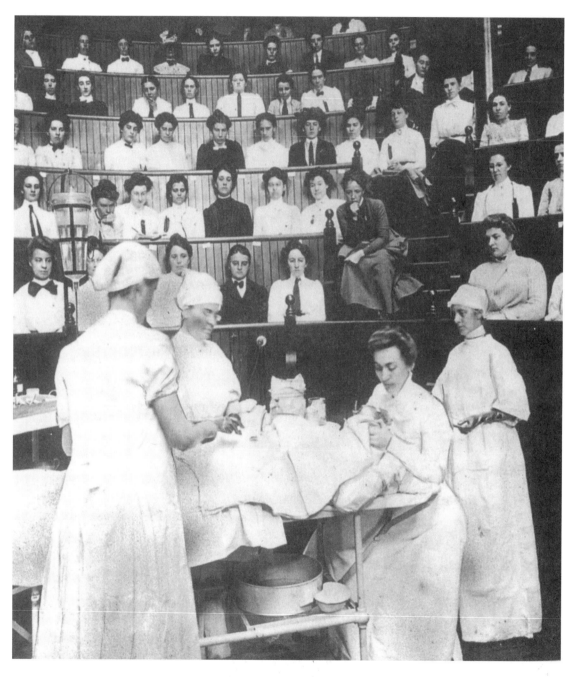

Human Research Subjects in Medicine

A hotly debated subject during the early 1900s revolved around the issue of using human subjects for medical experimentation. The term for using living humans or animals for study is "vivisection." Those opposed to the procedure (known as antivivesectionists) objected to procedures that did not offer a direct benefit to the human or animal subject's health. Several pieces of legislation advocating legal limits on animal and human research were proposed, but they were defeated. The issue ignited much controversy, as arsonists destroyed a New Jersey facility that bred research animals. The controversy raged throughout the twentieth century. Antivivesectionists proclaimed that the procedures were cruel to animals and the humans used for experimentation. They clashed with doctors who have argued in favor of animal testing and the use of corpses in the study of anatomy.

doctors were practicing medicine in 1900; one hundred of those were black. Most female physicians of the early 1900s operated private practices that served a largely female clientele.

Despite their small numbers, female physicians of the era were able to make significant contributions that benefited all people. Extraordinary women doctors of the early twentieth century include: Dorothy R. Mendenhall, who demonstrated in 1901 that Hodgkin's disease (a type of cancer) was not a form of tuberculosis; Mathilde A. Evans, an African American who founded the first hospital for blacks in Columbia, South Carolina; and Martha Wollstein, who conducted early studies of polio (along with Simon Flexner) in 1907. Despite these accomplishments, and those of thousands of other female physicians, male doctors were slow to fully accept women doctors as equals. Nevertheless, by the end of the twentieth century women comprised 50 percent of all medical students in America and held many of the nation's most prestigious medical posts.

As more and more people were trained as physicians, medical education became more rigorous. The AMA voted in 1900 to strengthen the requirements necessary to become a physician. The association advocated requiring four years of training for their new members. In 1906, the AMA and other concerned grouped banded together to form the Council

OPPOSITE PAGE
Female students watch a surgical operation demonstration in 1907.

on Medical Education, which was charged with inspecting and rating medical schools. The committee reported that 20 percent of the nation's centers for medical education were inadequate. In 1907, Abraham Flexner (1866–1959) was hired to write a detailed analysis on the state of American medical education. He spent several years in the field and issued a scathing report in 1910. He stated that many medical schools were in horrendous condition. Laboratories and surgical rooms were often filthy, medical libraries were often bare, and many medical professors did little class instruction. Flexner then convinced the Rockefeller Foundation to donate $50 million to fund those medical schools that functioned satisfactorily. Poor medical institutions around the United States were closed and well-run schools were strengthened through Flexner's efforts.

❖ MAJOR DISEASES OF THE 1900S

Many diseases that raged throughout the early 1900s and destroyed countless lives have been cured and largely forgotten by contemporary Americans. The most prevalent and insidious maladies of the era included pellagra, plague, tuberculosis, and yellow fever.

Pellagra is a terrible disease that is rare today, even in developing countries, but it was a major problem in the United States during the early 1900s. Caused by poor nutrition, pellagra results specifically from a lack of nicotinamide (a B vitamin), which causes inflammation of the skin (dermatitis), diarrhea, dementia, and often death. Unknown in America during the nineteenth century, pellagra was first noticed in several rural southern regions in 1902. By 1908, the disease had spread so quickly that Columbia, South Carolina, hosted a National Conference on Pellagra. By 1924, pellagra had been identified in thirty-six states, with more than 90 percent of all cases located in just nine southern states.

Pellagra was most prevalent in the southeastern United States, where many people's diets consisted mainly of fatty meats, cornmeal, and molasses. The disease spread as new corn milling techniques, which caused many vital nutrients to be removed, were gaining widespread acceptance. Residents in insane asylums often were afflicted with pellagra because their diet was extremely heavy in mass-produced cornmeal. Rural citizens who ground their own corn, on the other hand, were much less likely to have deficient diets and develop pellagra.

Many physicians and scientists worked valiantly to halt the spread of pellagra, but they remained largely unsuccessful for several decades. One of the primary reasons for the pellagra epidemic was the reaction of south-

*Houses infected by the
bubonic plague are
burned.* **Reproduced by
permission of Photo
Researchers, Inc.**

ern political, cultural, and business leaders. They were embarrassed by
their region's poverty, which contributed to the disease. Only continued
public outcries for action forced these officials to take a strong stance
against pellagra. The epidemic lasted until the 1940s. During that time,
pellagra is said to have appeared in more than three million Americans
and caused approximately one hundred thousand deaths.

Bubonic plague was another disease that threatened Americans during the early 1900s. Known since biblical times, the plague had been
stricking various regions around the world for more than fifteen hundred
years. In the early 1900s the disease, which is caused by the *Yersinia
pestis* bacillus and spread to humans by fleas from infected rats, hit twice
San Francisco. In 1900, a dead Chinese worker was discovered in the
basement of the Globe Hotel. Quickly, twelve blocks of the city's popular
Chinatown district were quarantined as police surrounded the area and
searched for infected people. Only twenty-two plague victims were discovered, however, as many Chinese immigrants hid from the authorities
out of fears of deportation. This initial San Francisco bubonic plague epidemic lasted until 1904. The community was divided between medical
officials, who insisted the disease was widespread, and the city's political
and business communities, who denied the existence of the plague. They
feared news of the disease would deter tourists and consumers from visit-
ing San Francisco. It was not until 1903, when more than one hundred
confirmed cases of the disease had been reported, that the state's elected
representatives took action. Newly elected Governor George C. Pardee, a
physician sympathetic to issues affecting public health, began an extensive campaign to eradicate the disease from San Francisco. He authorized

Typhoid Mary

Irish immigrant Mary Mallon (c. 1870–1938) spent most of the early 1900s working as a cook for several wealthy New York families. During much of this period, Mallon was infected with typhoid fever, a horrible disease that causes inflammation of the intestines, coughing, fever, abdominal pain, and diarrhea. Although she never came down with symptoms herself, Mallon was a carrier who spread the fever wherever she went. She was directly responsible for three deaths and fifty-three cases of the disease, and she may have been responsible for as many as fourteen hundred cases of typhoid in Ithaca, New York, in 1903. Mary Mallon was America's first identified carrier of typhoid. She gained international notoriety for spreading sickness and earned the infamous nickname "Typhoid Mary." She finally was persuaded to enter a hospital in 1907, and remained there until 1910. In 1914, hospital officials built a cottage for her at the Riverside Hospital in the Bronx, where she was quarantined for life. She died in 1938.

the demolition of decaying buildings that housed the rats that spread the plague. Although these efforts were largely successful, the 1906 San Francisco earthquake created excellent conditions for the plague to reappear. Several cases were confirmed in 1907, but the city's officials had learned from their previous mistakes with the earlier outbreak. Federal, state, and local officials and community leaders quickly banded together to aggressively battle the plague.

Another ancient disease that caused much concern in the early 1900s was tuberculosis. It is caused by a bacterial infection contracted by humans either from inhaling the bacteria or by eating meat from infected animals. The common symptoms of tuberculosis include coughing, fatigue, and weight loss. The bacteria most frequently attack the lungs. When an infected person coughs, the tubercles (nodules the body forms around the bacteria as a defense mechanism) burst and particles are expelled or released. People infected with tuberculosis can carry the disease for months or years. Little could be done for those afflicted with the disease in the early 1900s. The primary treatment consisted of rest and good nutrition, which only the wealthy could afford. The disease was a major American health crisis and accounted for more than 10 percent of all deaths from disease in 1908.

Public health efforts against tuberculosis began as early as 1889, when the New York City Board of Health recommended disinfecting the homes of people suffering from the malady. In 1904, scientists, doctors, and concerned citizens gathered in Philadelphia to form the National Association for the Study and Prevention of Tuberculosis. Led by Lawrence Flick, the group campaigned tirelessly to inform the public about the medical and financial costs of tuberculosis. They told how families could be devastated if an infected parent became too sick to work. Orphanages across America were filled with children whose parents had succumbed to the dreaded disease. One of the most effective means of raising awareness of the disease was through the sale of stamps called Christmas Seals. Journalist Jacob Riis (1849–1914) first advocated selling these stamps to raise funds to combat tuberculosis in 1907. The idea gained widespread acceptance in communities throughout the United States, as money poured in to pay for educational and health programs. Still, tuberculosis remained prevalent in America until the 1940s.

Journalist Jacob Riis first advocated selling stamps to raise funds to combat tuberculosis in 1907.

It took decades of heroic efforts from thousands of people before tuberculosis could be defeated. The strategies for eliminating tuberculosis became a model for other public health crises during the century. The fight against this disease demonstrated that the combined efforts of health officials, elected representatives, and enlightened citizens could be used to confront a major health scare effectively. The National Association for the Study and Prevention of Tuberculosis continues its efforts in the new millennium as the American Lung Association.

Yellow fever was another disease that had caused panic throughout the world for generations. Producing ghastly symptoms, yellow fever had resulted in many deaths. Victims suffer from headaches, fever, liver damage, and internal bleeding. Liver damage can cause jaundice, and internal bleeding results in a discharge from the nose and mouth, bloody stools, and black vomit.

Yellow fever outbreaks caused mass panics throughout the nation, as communities feared the rapid and unpredictable spread of the disease. Quarantines were established, better sewer and water treatment facilities

Medical Quacks

Among the biggest medical problems of the early 1900s were hucksters and con men who traveled throughout the country selling tonics and elixirs that promised to cure nearly every known disease, pain, and sickness. One of the most famous cure-alls was "Mary's Wonderful Stomach Remedy," which was sold to relieve appendicitis, gallstones, liver problems, and stomach ailments. The "remedy" was composed only of olive oil and salt. Many of the other tonics sold in the early 1900s contained large quantities of alcohol and opium. Writer Samuel Hopkins Adams was one of the leading voices crusading against this medical quackery. In 1905, he published a famous article in *McClure's* magazine that exposed these fraudulent cures to the public. The American Medical Association also spoke out against these phony physicians and their fake cures with some success. Many hucksters were driven out of business, but the problem of quack medicine lingered throughout the decade.

were built to reduce the mosquitoes' habitat, and public health boards were established to deal with afflicted citizens. In 1881, Carlos Finlay first proposed the theory that mosquitoes were the agents of the dreaded sickness. By 1900, Finlay was advising the federal government as a member of the U.S. Army Yellow Fever Commission, which had been organized to combat the disease during the Spanish-American War (1898). The last yellow fever outbreak in the United States occurred in New Orleans in 1905. By the end of the decade, the nation's federal, state, and local governments were dedicated to controlling the mosquito population through extensive use of pesticides and other toxic chemicals. While these tactics solved the yellow fever problem, the heavy use of chemicals would cause further health problems later in the century.

Hookworm was another aggressive disease that debilitated citizens in the early 1900s. Most common in the rural South, the hookworm thrived in unsanitary conditions such as those present in outhouses. The parasite often would infect people who walked through larvae-filled soil in bare feet. Those afflicted developed such symptoms as dry hair, ulcerated skin and feet, protruding shoulder blades and stomachs, and diminished physical and mental energy. These symptoms contributed to the cultural stereotype of the barefoot, lazy, and slow-witted Southerner. Hookworm was eventually eradicated through the efforts of Charles Wardell Stiles (1867–1941), a zoologist who noticed similarities in hookworm diseases suffered by animals and people. He announced the causes of the ailment and outlined a plan to defeat hookworm. In 1909, industrialist John D. Rockefeller (1839–1937) donated $1 million to fund the Rockefeller Sanitary Commission, which aided hundreds of thousands of hookworm sufferers. By 1914, hookworm had been banished from most states.

For More Information

BOOKS

Bryan, Jenny. *The History of Health and Medicine.* New York: Thomson Learning Center, 1996.

Casanelles, Antonio, and Ali Garousi. *Great Discoveries and Inventions That Improved Human Health.* New York: Gareth Stevens, 2000.

DeJaurengui, Ruth. *100 Medical Milestones That Shaped World History.* San Mateo, CA: Bluewood Books, 1998.

Fradin, Dennis Brindell. *We Have Conquered Pain: The Discovery of Anesthesia.* New York: Margaret McElderry, 1996.

Franck, Irene, and David Brownstone. *Healers: Work Throughout History.* New York: Facts on File, Inc.

Hoff, Brent. *Mapping Epidemics: A Historical Atlas of Diseases.* New York: Franklin Watts, Inc., 2000.

Kratoville, Betty Lou. *Great Medical Milestones.* New York: Academic Therapy Publications, 1999.

Lamond, Margrete. *Plague and Pestilence: Deadly Diseases That Changed the World.* New York: Allen & Unwin, 1997.

Miller, Brandon Marie. *Just What the Doctor Ordered: The History of American Medicine.* Minneapolis: Lerner Publications, 1997.

Parker, Steve. *Medical Advances (20th Century Inventions).* Austin, TX: Raintree, 1998.

Ritchie, David, and Fred Israel, Linda Leuzzi, and DeWayne Pickles. *Health and Medicine: Life in America 100 Years Ago.* New York: Chelsea House, 1995.

Senior, Kathryn. *Medicine: Doctors, Demons, and Drugs.* New York: Franklin Watts, Inc., 1997.

Tiner, John. *100 Scientists Who Shaped World History.* San Mateo, CA: Bluewood Books, 2000.

Yount, Lisa. *Disease Detectives.* San Diego, CA: Lucent Books, 2000.

Yount, Lisa. *The History of Medicine.* San Diego, CA: Lucent Books, 2001.

Yount, Lisa. *Medical Technology.* New York: Facts on File, 1998.

WEB SITES

Acheivements in Public Health, 1900–1999: Changes in the Public Health System. http://www.cdc.gov/mmwr/preview/mmwrhtml/mm4850a1.htm (accessed on August 8, 2002).

Health Sentinel—Vaccines. http://www.healthsentinel.com/Vaccines/Vaccines.htm (accessed on August 8, 2002).

Medicine and Madison Avenue—Timeline. http://scriptorium.lib.duke.edu/mma/timeline.html#1900 (accessed on August 8, 2002).

Vim & Vigor Library—How Health Changed. http://www.vigormagazine.com/lib/Kid/Kid-How_Health_Changed.htm (accessed on August 8, 2002).

chapter seven **Science and Technology**

1900: Thomas Alva Edison invents the nickel-based alkaline storage battery.

1900: German scientists invent the modern pendulum seismograph to detect earthquakes.

1900: Sigmund Freud's *On the Interpretation of Dreams* is published.

1900: July 2 The first Zeppelin dirigible is flown in Germany.

1900: December 14 Max Planck, a German physicist, announces the basis of quantum theory: Light rays are emitted in discrete amounts called quanta.

1901: General Electric establishes the first corporate research laboratory.

1901: Andrew Carnegie announces his intention to donate $10 million to promote scientific research.

1901: Brothers Orville and Wilbur Wright begin glider flights to study the aerodynamics of flight.

1901: Hugo de Vries, a Dutch biologist, publishes his theory of genetic mutation.

1901: December 12 Guglielmo Marconi receives the first transatlantic radio transmission.

1902: The lawn mower and vacuum cleaner are invented in England.

1902: Arthur Korn, a German inventor, develops the photofacsimile machine, which transmits photographs by telegraph.

1902: Ivan Pavlov, a Russian physiologist and psychologist, discovers conditioned reflexes.

1902: Richard Zsigmondy, a German chemist, invents the ultramicroscope.

1902: British physicists Ernest Rutherford and Frederick Soddy explain radioactivity as the disintegration of atomic structures.

1903: Reginald Fessenden discovers the electrolytic radio detector, a machine capable of receiving the human voice.

1903: The safety razor is invented

1903: Edison perfects a technique for producing master record molds, called electroplating.

1903: Bertrand Russell, an English philosopher, publishes *The Principles of Mathematics,* which attempts to reduce pure mathematics to a limited number of concepts.

1903: December 17 The Wright brothers successfully take flight at Kitty Hawk, North Carolina.

1904: The Panama Canal construction project begins.

1904: John Fleming invents the diode vacuum tube, which converts an alternating electric current into a one-way signal.

1904: Charles Perrine discovers the sixth moon of Jupiter.

1904: Phonograph records replace Edison's wax cylinders in sound recording.

1904: The United States Engineering Society is founded.

1905: Albert Einstein publishes several important papers on the theory of relativity, Brownian motion, and the photoelectric effect.

1905: German physicist Philipp Lenard is awarded the Nobel Prize in physics for his discovery of cathode rays.

1905: The German Navy launches the first U-boat submarine.

1905: Ernest Starling, an English physiologist, coins the term "hormone" to identify chemical messengers produced by the endocrine glands.

1906: Thaddeus Cahill invents telharmonium, a type of telephonic organ.

1906: The Nobel Prize in physics is awarded to scientist J.J. Thomson for his discovery of the electron.

1906: December 24 The first radio broadcast originates from Brant Rock, Massachusetts.

1906: December 31 Lee De Forest invents the triode vacuum tube, which made possible the transmission of human voice, music, and other broadcast signals via wireless telephony.

1907: The first helicopter flight takes place in France.

1907: Albert Michelson becomes the first American Nobel laureate when he wins the Nobel Prize in physics for measuring the speed of light.

1908: The electric razor is invented.

1908: George Ellery Hale discovers magnetic fields in sunspots.

1908: The Ford Motor Company introduces the Model T, or "Tin Lizzie," the most popular of the early automobiles.

1908: Dutch physicist Heike Kamerlingh Onnes produces liquid helium.

1908: The Holt Company introduces the first tractor with moving treads.

1908: December 21 Wilbur Wright flies seventy-seven miles in two hours and twenty minutes, winning the Michelin Cup in France.

1909: The terms *gene, genotype,* and *phenotype* are introduced by biologist Wilhelm Johannsen.

1909: April 6 U.S. Navy commander Robert Peary reaches the North Pole.

1909: September Psychoanalyst Sigmund Freud makes his only visit to the United States, to lecture at Clark University in Worcester, Massachusetts.

1909: November 24 Celebrations in England and the United States mark the fiftieth anniversary of the publication of Charles Darwin's *On the Origins of Species* and the centennial of Darwin's birth.

Overview

Scientific and technological advancements invented and perfected during the early 1900s had significant effects throughout the twentieth century. Intense thought, research, and experimentation in the fields of mechanics, communications, physics, genetics, and psychology dominated the decade. Scientists in America and around the world worked to develop breakthroughs that would enhance the quality of human life.

The three most important inventions developed during the decade included the automobile, the airplane, and the radio. Each new device transformed American life by greatly expanding the average citizen's opportunities for travel and communication. Henry Ford and other Americans improved the automobile, which had been invented in Germany. Soon the United States was covered with paved roads, and people were able to travel great distances in a swift and affordable manner. No other technological achievement of the early 1900s captured the public's imagination more than the airplane. The ability of humans to take flight symbolized the unlimited potential of the dawning century. Radio, which had evolved from advances in telegraph and telephone technology, was a revolutionary step forward in communications because, unlike its predecessors, it did not require wires.

Discoveries in science and technology during the 1900s were shared internationally. A breakthrough announced in one nation was quickly followed by an exchange of ideas and theories from around the globe. Scientists and inventors in other countries offered suggestions for possible improvements and notions for building upon the initial idea. The automobile owes its creation to inventors primarily in Germany, France, and the United States. The race to invent the airplane was mainly between the Wright brothers of Ohio and their counterparts in France. A combination of American, Italian, English, and Croatian scientists were responsible for the birth of radio.

While American technology advanced rapidly during the early 1900s, American science did not keep pace. In the late nineteenth century, there were only a few thousand American research scientists working throughout the nation. University programs stressing theoretical research grew very slowly because professors favored sciences with more practical applications, such as agriculture and engineering. Although the United States lagged behind Europe in scientific achievements, the country's best thinkers closely followed the breakthroughs of their foreign counterparts. For example, American biologists and plant and animal breeders carefully watched the developments in the new science of genetics, which had grown from the discoveries of Gregor Mendel and others. Great European minds such as Albert Einstein and Sigmund Freud introduced their theories during the decade inspiring thinkers around the world. American astronomers participated in international space research and made significant contributions to the field from their home observatories. One of the most significant changes in science was greater emphasis on research for its own sake in universities and laboratories across the nation. Scientists were now encouraged to probe the mysteries of the physical world, not just to solve practical concerns, but also to focus on pure research to benefit humanity.

Luther Burbank (1848–1926) Luther Burbank is one of America's most renowned botanists. Largely self-taught, Burbank was heavily influenced by Charles Darwin's research into hybridization, or how breeders could develop better specimens of plants and animals. He began experimenting with growing improved varieties of vegetables. His most successful experiment was the Burbank potato hybrid. Burbank gained national prominence through his popular plant catalogues and writings on hybridization. *Photograph reproduced by permission of the Corbis Corporation.*

Lee De Forest (1873–1961) Lee De Forest is known as "the father of radio" for his invention of the audion in 1906. The audion generated, amplified, and detected radio signals, making it possible to transmit the human voice and other broadcasts via wireless telephony. De Forest used his invention to make numerous important broadcasts during the following decade, such as the first transmission of live music in 1910 and the first radio news report in 1916. In the 1920s De Forest developed a sound process for motion pictures called Phonofilm, but it failed commercially due to Hollywood's commitment to silent movies. De Forest patented three hundred inventions during his career.

Thomas Alva Edison (1847–1931) Ohio native Thomas Alva Edison, who received only three months of formal education in his lifetime, is hailed as one of the most important inventors in human history. In 1876, he opened a laboratory in Menlo Park, New Jersey, in which he created hundreds of his inventions. The following year, he invented the phonograph and gained international acclaim. Edison's most noteworthy experimentation produced the incandescent light bulb in 1879. During his long career, Edison received more than one thousand patents on numerous inventions related to such diverse technologies as motion pictures, batteries, and automobiles. *Photograph reproduced by permission of Archive Photos, Inc.*

George Ellery Hale (1868–1938) To astrophysicist George Ellery Hale, more powerful telescopes were key to finding out the physical nature of celestial bodies. With the help of others, including the Carnegie Institution, he was able to build increasingly large instruments that repeatedly surpassed all others in focal length and light-gathering power. Using a sixty-inch telescope on top of Mount Wilson near Pasadena, California, he discovered that sunspots are cooler than other regions of the Sun and also possess intense magnetic firelds. These were the most significant discoveries regarding sunspots since Galileo first discovered them in the seventeenth century. *Photograph reproduced by permission of Archive Photos, Inc.*

Granville Stanley Hall (1844–1924) Granville Stanley Hall pioneered "scientific" psychology, the theory that human mental and emotional states were based completely on physiology. In 1884 he established the first experimental psychology laboratory in the United States at Johns Hopkins University, where he researched how physical sensations triggered mental perceptions and emotions. Hall also conducted extensive investigations into hypnosis and the unconscious mind, and he later studied developmental psychology in children. One of the founders of the American Psychological Association, he served as the organization's first president. *Photograph reproduced by permission of the Corbis Corporation.*

Albert Abraham Michelson (1852–1931) Physicist Albert Abraham Michelson dedicated his professional life to researching the speed of light and devising a means to measure it accurately. In 1881, he invented the interferometer, which studied the nature and behavior of light waves. In 1887, Michelson worked with fellow physicist Edward Morely on a famous experiment in which they proved light could be detected regardless of a light beam's rotation. This experiment served as a significant basis for Albert Einstein's theory of relativity. In 1907, Michelson was the first American to be awarded a Nobel Prize for his advances in optical measuring instruments, meteorology, and spectroscopy. *Photograph courtesy of the Library of Congress.*

Robert Edwin Peary (1856–1920) Explorer Robert Edwin Peary began his career in 1886 when he journeyed to Greenland on a self-designed, one-man sled. He traveled around the area's Mount Wistar, which is now called Peary Land. Subsequent treks through the region made him an international celebrity. Peary confirmed Greenland was an island in 1895. In 1898, he began a five-year leave of absence from the U.S. Navy to explore the Arctic. Peary's ambition was to lead the first expedition to the North Pole. He reached the Pole on his eighth and final attempt, on April 6, 1909. *Photograph reproduced by permisssion of the Corbis Corporation.*

Wilbur (1867–1912) and Orville (1871–1948) Wright In the late 1890s the Wright brothers became intrigued with aeronautics and began to study the principles of flight by using gliders. After several years of study, experimentation, and construction, the Wright brothers designed a glider with a twelve-horsepower engine and propellers turned with bicycle chains. On December 17, 1903, Orville made humankind's first successful flight, 852 feet in fifty-nine seconds. The Wright brothers improved their designs and were awarded a U.S. patent for their "flying machine" in 1906. Soon the British, French, and American governments entered into negotiations with the Wright brothers to manufacture aircraft and train pilots.

◆◆ *Topics in the News* ....

❖ THE AUTOMOBILE

Gottleib Daimler (1834–1900) and Karl Benz (1844–1929) crafted the first modern automobile in the late nineteenth century in Germany. Daimler first developed his gasoline engine to be used on a four-wheeled vehicle in 1886, and by the 1890s the two men had begun production on their motorcars in France. However, it would be American industrialist Henry Ford (1863–1947) who truly revolutionized the auto industry. Unlike other automakers in the United States, who were designing large models for the wealthy, Ford envisioned creating practical vehicles that everyone could afford. The Quadricycle, Ford's first car, was built in 1896. A few years later,

he founded the Ford Motor Company, and by 1904 the corporation was producing twenty-five cars each day. The most successful of Ford's early models was the Model T (nicknamed the "Tin Lizzie"), which had an engine comprised of four cylinders cast together in a single block. This innovation remains the basic design of the internal combustion engine. The Model T also featured a new transmission with three pedals, one to move forward, one to move backward, and one to brake. Thousands of Model Ts were sold in 1909, its first year of production. The car was so popular that by the end of World War I (1914–18), half the automobiles in the world were Model Ts.

Henry Ford was not the nation's sole automaker; he faced several major U.S. competitors. Ransom Eli Olds manufactured his first "Merry Oldsmobile" in 1896, while the Stanley brothers of Newton, Massachusetts, created a steam-driven car (the Stanley Steamer) in 1897. Between 1900 and 1908, 502 automobile companies were established, of which 302 failed. One of the more successful carmakers of the era was David D. Buick, whose company became the leading auto producer in 1908. That same year, Buick merged with Olds and Cadillac (two other independent companies) to form the General Motors Company. Another of America's leading auto corporations was formed in 1908, when Walter Chrysler introduced his first model.

The invention of the automobile had an immediate and dramatic impact upon the nation's lifestyle. The first major cultural shift was the rapid reduction in horse-drawn transportation. Fewer horses resulted in less manure and cleaner urban streets. Health care was improved, as physicians could make house calls to remote communities with greater ease and speed. American roads soon were filled with a variety of motor vehicles, including ambulances, postal cars, and delivery trucks, which further improved the quality of life. Throughout the decade, international interest in automobiles also increased. Technological improvements in design and mechanics stimulated worldwide consumer interest in the transportation marvel.

❖ THE AIRPLANE

The history of American aviation begins in the nineteenth century with ballooning. During the Civil War, both the Union and Confederate armies used balloons for reconnaissance missions to observe enemy troop movements. Many people throughout the world believed dirigibles (gas-powered balloons) would serve as the primary means of air travel in the future. Others, however, were convinced manned flight would come about only through mechanical innovation. One of the earliest proponents of the new science of aeronautical engineering was Samuel P. Langley (1834–1906), director of the Smithsonian Institution. Langley began working with model airplanes in the 1880s. In 1896, one of his models flew

OPPOSITE PAGE
The Model T. **Reproduced by permission of the National Automobile Museum.**

three thousand feet along the Potomac River. Another aviation pioneer was French-born engineer Octave Chanute (1832–1910), who experimented with piloting gliders. Chanute had a major success in 1896, when he registered a glide of 256 feet during a test on the Indiana shore of Lake Michigan. Langley, Chanute, and many others worked tirelessly to become the first human to take flight. A national frenzy was created as journalists reported on the inventors' race to fly. In 1903, Langley built an airplane called the *Aerodrome,* which had a five-cylinder engine, but it was a failure. Only nine days after Langley's ill-fated attempts to fly, Orville and Wilbur Wright became the first humans to achieve engine-powered flight at Kitty Hawk, North Carolina. Their effort succeeded in large part because the brothers had focused on the interaction between the wing and air currents before designing their motorized glider.

In 1907, several years after the Wright brothers' historic achievement, inventor Alexander Graham Bell (1847–1922) established the Aerial Experiment Association (AEA). He was convinced that the Wrights' plane was extremely dangerous because it needed high speeds to take off and maintain flight. Bell experimented with a piloted flying kite that would travel only 15 miles per hour, but this prototype failed. Another member of the AEA, Thomas Selfridge, made history by becoming the first Ameri-

Aviation pioneers Wilbur and Orville Wright in their first airplane. ***Courtesy of the Library of Congress.***

The creation of radio is due in large measure to the work of two scientists: Guglielmo Marconi and Nikola Tesla (1856–1943). Tesla, a Croatian-born physicist, had immigrated to the United States in 1884 and had spent several years working on alternating current electrical systems for Thomas Edison. In 1893 he gave an influential lecture in St. Louis, Missouri, predicting wireless telegraphy based on spark transmission. Two years later another physicist, the Italian-born Marconi, was hailed as the discoverer of radiotelegraphy through his work with spark transmissions. Marconi insisted that he had invented the new technology independently, and he had been unaware of Tesla's remarks. The two inventors became embroiled in litigation over patent infringement for several years. Marconi's original patent was eventually disallowed, but his claim to being the "father of radio" remains, due to the fact he actually developed wireless telegraphy while Tesla's research was more theoretical. Still, Tesla's 1904 prediction that radio would someday "prove very efficient in enlightening the masses, particularly in still-uncivilized countries and less accessible regions, and that it will add materially to general safety, comfort, and convenience and maintenance of peaceful relations" was correct. Radio's discovery and evolution during the early 1900s paved the way for mass communication and an emerging "global village" later in the century.

can aviation casualty when he was killed in a crash while flying with Orville Wright. Despite these setbacks, aviation captured the public's imagination as a marvel of the modern age. By the conclusion of the first decade of the 1900s, the Wrights and others were manufacturing airplanes for both military and civilian use. In the 1910s, the airplane would see further innovations as production expanded during World War I.

❖ THE RADIO

The history of radio began in 1887, when German physicist Heinrich Hertz (1857–1894) produced electromagnetic waves from an oscillating circuit connected to an induction coil. Soon "Hertzian waves" were being studied in laboratories throughout the world. In 1895, Italian physicist Guglielmo Marconi (1874–1937) discovered that he was able to send Morse code

A young Guglielmo Marconi seated behind his electrical apparatus.
Reproduced by permission of the Corbis Corporation.

signals through the air. Marconi soon was joined in his studies by English physicist Oliver Lodge. Together they learned how to transmit waves of a definite length and created a receiver that could be tuned to waves of specific lengths. This discovery is now recognized as the first radio. On December 12, 1901, Marconi received history's first transatlantic wireless message, in Morse code, on his antenna at Cape Cod, Massachusetts.

The earliest radio instruments were unable to transmit the human voice. They were actual wireless telegraphs, in that they could receive only dots and dashes produced by electrified oscillations. The early 1900s was a decade during which several prominent scientists, including Marconi, Reginald Fessenden, and Lee De Forest, raced to be the first to successfully transmit the human voice. A true breakthrough occurred in 1906 with De Forest's invention of the triode vacuum tube, or audion, which was based on earlier works by Edison and John Fleming. De Forest found a means to gain greater clarity and strength when receiving radio signals by adding a third electrode to the two-electrode vacuum tube. Another advance in radio's evolution happened that same year, when Henry Dunwoody, an army general, discovered that carborundum crystals could detect electrical currents. Dunwoody's work set in motion the development of crystal receivers, which would be employed on thousands of homemade radio sets in later decades.

It would not be until the 1910s that modern broadcasting would begin. In 1912, entrepreneur David Sarnoff (1891–1971) received wireless distress messages from the *Titanic* ocean liner as the doomed ship was sinking following its collision with an iceberg. Sarnoff broadcast the messages by voice to retail stores owned by John Wanamaker, who earlier had installed a radio to lure customers. The incident captivated the public and made people aware of the great possibilities inherent in radio for disseminating news and entertainment. In 1916, Sarnoff joined forces with Marconi to manufacture a "Radio Music Box," priced at approximately seventy-five dollars each. By 1919, the Marconi Company had merged with General Electric to form the Radio Corporation of America (RCA). Sarnoff became RCA's first president. Its primary rival was Westinghouse Electric, which began operating the first commercially profitable radio broadcasting station (KDKA in Pittsburgh) in November 1920. Radio would come to dominate American culture during the 1920s.

❖ THE BUILDING BLOCKS OF LIFE

American achievements in the field of biology during the 1900s were based on the scientific advances of the late nineteenth century. Much of the period's interest in biology centered on the study of genetics and the possibility of altering the genetic makeup of cells and organisms. German-born biologist Jacques Loeb (1859–1924) pioneered experimentation with parthenogenesis, the process of stimulating an egg to develop into an organism without being fertilized. Loeb believed life could be engineered, and he promoted the notion that life could eventually be created in a test tube. Critics labeled him "Dr. Frankenstein" for his manipulations of life and reproduction. His legacy can be found in the research of many later American scientists, such as John Watson and B. F. Skinner, who were influenced by Loeb's theories that life could be created, predicted, and controlled by scientific methods.

Another nineteenth-century pioneer in biology was Gregor Mendel, an Austrian monk whose experiments with plant hybrids in the 1850s and 1860s revealed the existence of dominant parental characteristics in subsequent generations of particular life forms. He discovered hereditary determinants, which he classified as either dominant (controlling the next generation's physical appearance) or recessive (not producing an apparent trait but still inherited by offspring). Little attention was paid to Mendel's discoveries until 1900, when three European biologists—Hugo de Vries, Karl Correns, and Erich von Tschmeak—independently rediscovered the monk's theories. In 1909, Danish biologist Wilhelm Johannsen coined the term *gene* to represent the primary unit of heredity. Americans also showed much interest in Mendel's work during the early 1900s, as breeders reasoned that his findings made it possible for them to predict the

Antivivisectionism

Vivisection involves the experimental use of living animals to observe physiological processes under laboratory conditions. Most physiology and endocrinology researchers performed the technique during the late nineteenth and early twentieth centuries. They believed studying the bodily functions of animal subjects was necessary to provide better health care for humans. The movement to limit experimental animal testing began in Europe in the 1870s. The American Antivivisection Society was founded in Philadelphia, Pennsylvania, in 1883. Protests against the cruelty to animals in the name of science roared during the first decade of the 1900s, alarming the research community. In their view, antivivisectionsectionists seemed to be threatening the unprecedented advances that medical science had made in the preceding decades. Scientists saw animal testing as vital to expanding knowledge in many areas, including the digestive, cardiovascular, and nervous systems. The antivivisection movement revealed the public's interest in medical ethics. The debate on the merits of vivisection continues into the new millennium.

probable outcomes of specific breeding strategies. One area where Mendel's research proved to be an invaluable aide was in the study of the structure and functions of chromosomes. Columbia University graduate students Walter Sutton and W.A. Cannon were the first to hypothesize that the division of chromosomes might be the mechanism that explained Mendelian segregation. Their hypothesis was supported by findings reported in 1905 by scientists E. B. Wilson at Columbia and Nettie Stevens at Bryn Mawr University. Working independently, Wilson and Stevens each demonstrated that while all eggs possess a single X chromosome, each sperm may carry either an X or a Y chromosome. Consequently, cells in females contain two X chromosomes, and those of males have one X chromosome and one Y chromosome.

Many of the decade's laboratory experiments in genetics were conducted on the common fruit fly, *Drosophila melanogaster.* Scientists chose to use these flies because they have a short reproductive cycle (ten days to three weeks), produce numerous offspring (one hundred to more than four hundred in each generation), and possess only a few chromosomes. One of the most prominent researchers to experiment with the flies was Thomas Hunt

Morgan (1866–1945). He theorized that they might be helpful in testing Charles Darwin's ideas of natural selection. To accomplish his goal, Morgan developed a new type of experimental research called "microevolution," which combines concepts surrounding mutation and variation. The work of Morgan and others led directly to the "synthetic theory of evolution," which has dominated biological studies since the 1930s. According to this viewpoint, natural selection is seen as acting on gene pools, rather than on individuals. Thus, Darwin's theories on evolution are now understood through the lens of Mendel's work in genetics.

❖ UNDERSTANDING DREAMS

Sigmund Freud, an Austrian psychiatrist, had a tremendous impact on the twentieth century due to his theory on the psychology of human behavior. Freud stated that human behavior is based upon the workings of the unconscious mind. In his landmark text, *On the Interpretation of Dreams* (1900), Freud outlined his revolutionary theory. According to Freud, people often repress unpleasant thoughts and emotions, but these feelings are not totally eliminated. Rather, the negative thoughts reappear in the unconscious mind and are revealed to the person, in a distorted form, as dreams. Freud believed the key to understanding a person's unconscious fears and desires was through analysis of their dreams. Once a dream was analyzed, the doctor would assist the patient in reconstructing his or her past emotional life in order to understand the events or emotions that caused distress. According to Freud, many people's most commonly suppressed thoughts center on sexual matters. This belief scandalized many European physicians, who feared Freud was encouraging his patients' "perversity." For most of the early 1900s, Freud discussed his ideas with a small group of colleagues and students, as he was unwilling to face the hostility of the medical establishment.

Freud gained international fame in 1909, when he agreed to present his theories in a series of lectures at Clark University in Worchester, Massachusetts. Numerous leaders in American psychiatry, as well as other intellectuals, journeyed to New England to hear Freud speak during his only visit to the United States. In a series of five lectures, Freud offered a comprehensive explanation of his psychological system. He addressed numerous topics, including: the causes of and treatment for hysteria; the mechanism of repression; analysis of dreams and verbal mistakes (an incorrect word or image replaces a similar one, now referred to as "Freudian slips"); the sexuality of children; and the emotional demands of civilization. Freud's lectures sent an immediate shock wave through the American psychiatric and psychological communities. Some psychiatrists quickly adopted Freud's theories and strongly supported the idea of psychoanalysis. These physicians accepted Freud's notion that emotional problems are not the result of physical causes, but instead are rooted in the patient's own mind and experiences.

Much attention was given to Freud's idea that civilization's morality was at the root of many emotional disorders, since society advocated repressing sexual desires. The repression of one's sexual impulses, Freud explained, resulted in neurosis. While Freud was offering his theories, Victorian society's strict moral rules were being attacked by others as repressive, hypocritical, and unhealthy. Some progressive thinkers promoted sexual education as a result. Freud's theories not only changed the psychiatric profession, causing it to consider the role of the unconscious mind in people's behavior, but also spurred Americans to change their attitudes toward sex.

❖ ALBERT EINSTEIN'S THEORY OF RELATIVITY

The scientist who had perhaps the most lasting intellectual impact upon the twentieth century was a Jewish German theoretical physicist named Albert Einstein (1879–1955). In 1905, Einstein devised his special theory of

Austrian psychiatrist Sigmund Freud at work in his study. Reproduced by permission of Archive Photos, Inc.

ince the 1840s, primitive photographic technology had been used to examine solar eclipses. A great advance was made when Warren de la Rue invented the photoheliograph, a photographic telescope with a fast shutter that could map the surface of the sun. On August 30, 1905, hundreds of astronomers gathered in Spain to observe a total solar eclipse. Although they did not obtain significant data, American astronomers were present in large numbers and participated fully with their international counterparts in studying the event. Many scientific historians cite the 1905 eclipse as the moment when American astronomy came of age.

relativity. Einstein's theory dealt with uniform linear motion at constant but high velocities. He determined that the speed of light remains constant in a vacuum, independent of the light source or the observer, and that mass and energy are equivalent. His ideas on special relativity are a landmark in human thought and have become foundation for modern physics.

Einstein's most famous formula, "$E = mc^{2}$" (E represents energy, m is mass, and c is the speed of light) demonstrates that a small mass traveling at the speed of light is equivalent to a vast amount of energy. As a result of this equivalence, time and space are not absolute: What one person sees or measures may be different from that of another observer in a different frame of reference. Special relativity also debunks the existence of the ether, an invisible and undetectable substance that scientists had formerly believed filled the universe. In a famous paradox resulting from his theory, Einstein showed that time slows down at very high speeds. Consequently, an astronaut traveling through space for many years at speeds approaching that of light would discover upon his return to Earth that his twin would have become an elderly man while the astronaut would have hardly aged at all.

Many American scientists dismissed Einstein's revolutionary ideas as abstract, unworkable, or nonsensical. In 1914, Einstein expanded his concepts to include nonlinear motion in a general theory of relativity. This introduced his famous theory of curved space-time. In 1921, Einstein was awarded the Nobel Prize in physics for his study of the photoelectric effect. Although some aspects of his theories on relativity eventually were verified by other scientists, his research remained controversial for decades.

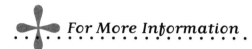 *For More Information*

BOOKS

Adair, Gene. *Thomas Alva Edison: Inventing the Electric Age.* New York: Oxford University Press, 1997.

Bendick, Jeanne, and Sal Murdocca. *Eureka! It's an Automobile.* Brookfield, CT: Millbrook Press, 1994.

Brailler, Jess. *Who Was Albert Einstein?* New York: Grosset and Dunlap, 2002.

Calvert, Patricia. *Robert Peary: To the Top of the World.* New York: Benchmark Books, 2001.

Carter, Alden. *Radio: From Marconi to the Space Age.* New York: Franklin Watts, 1987.

Freedman, Russell. *The Wright Brothers and How They Invented the Airplane.* New York: Holiday House, 1994.

Hammontree, Marie, and Robert Doremus. *Albert Einstein: Young Thinker.* New York: Aladdin Paperbacks, 1986.

Humble, Richard. *Submarines.* New York: Franklin Watts, 1985.

Miles, Lisa, and Alastair Smith. *The Usborne Complete Book of Astrology and Space.* Tulsa, OK: E.D.C. Publications, 1998.

Miller, Ray, and Glenn Embree. *Henry's Lady: An Illustrated History of the Model A Ford.* Oceanside. CA: Evergreen Press, 1972.

Murphy, Frank, and Dan Brown. *Always Inventing: The True Story of Thomas Alva Edison.* New York: Scholastic, 2002.

Quackenbush, Robert. *Here a Plant, There a Plant, Everywhere a Plant, Plant: A Story of Luther Burbank.* Englewood Cliffs, NJ: Prentice Hall, 1982.

Reef, Catherine. *Sigmund Freud: Pioneer of the Mind.* New York: Clarion Books, 2001.

Reynolds, Quentin. *The Wright Brothers: Pioneers of American Aviation.* New York: Random House, 1981.

Rozakis, Laurie. *Matthew Henson and Robert Peary: The Race for the North Pole.* New York: Blackbirch, 1994.

Vancleave, Janice. *Janice Vancleave's Biology for Every Kid: 101 Easy Experiments That Really Work.* New York: John Wiley & Sons, 1990.

Wills, Susan, Steven Wills, and Jenna Anderson, eds. *Looking at the Stars.* Minneapolis, MN: Oliver Press, 2001.

WEB SITES

Global Networking Timeline: 1900–1959. http://www.ciolek.com/PAPERS/GLOBAL/1900early.html (accessed on August 8, 2002).

Science History Timeline, After 1900. http://www.howe.k12.ok.us/~jimaskew/chistory.htm (accessed on August 8, 2002).

A Science Odyssey: Then + Now Menu. http://www.pbs.org/wgbh/aso/ thenandnow/ (accessed on August 8, 2002).

Twentieth Century Inventions 1900 to 1999—Inventors. http://inventors.about. com/library/weekly/aa121599a.htm?PM=ss11_inventors (accessed on August 8, 2002).

chapter eight *Sports*

1900: **January 29** In professional baseball, Byron Bancroft "Ban" Johnson forms the American League by expanding the former minor-league Western Association to include eastern cities.

1900: **April 19** James Caffrey wins the fourth Boston Marathon with a time of 2 hours, 39 minutes, and 44 seconds.

1900: **May 20-October 28** Paris, France, hosts the Summer Olympic Games, then called the International Meeting of Physical Training and Sport.

1901: **January 8-11** The American Bowling Congress holds the first national Bowling Championship in Chicago, Illinois. The total prize money is $1,592.

1901: **August 21** Joe "Iron Man" McGinty, a Baltimore Orioles pitcher, is expelled from major league baseball for stepping on an umpire's toes, spitting in his face, and punching him. McGinty is later reinstated due to an outcry from his fans.

1901: **September** The Pittsburgh Pirates win the National League pennant, while the Chicago White Sox capture the first American League pennant.

1902: **January 1** At the first Tournament of Roses Association football game, held in Pasadena, California, the University of Michigan defeats Stanford University by a score of 49-0. The Rose Bowl becomes an annual event in 1916.

1902: **August 8** The United States defeats Great Britain, three matches to two, to win a second consecutive Davis Cup.

1902: **September** The Pittsburgh Pirates win the National League pennant, while the Philadelphia Athletics win the American League pennant.

1902: **April 22** Jack Root defeats Charles "Kid" McCoy for the light heavyweight boxing title.

1902: **August 14** Jim Jeffries defeats James Corbett and retains his heavyweight boxing title.

1902: **October 1-13** In baseball's first World Series, Boston defeats Pittsburgh five games to three.

1902: **November** Harvard Stadium, the first stadium built specifically for football, is opened.

1904: **February 22** The National Ski Association holds the first national ski-jumping championship in Ishpeming, Michigan.

1904: **May 5** Denton "Cy" Young pitches the first perfect game under modern baseball rules, not allowing any opposing player to reach first base.

1904: **July 1-November 23** St. Louis, Missouri, hosts the Summer Olympic Games.

1905: American May Sutton becomes the first non-Briton to win the Wimbledon tennis championship, held at the All-England Club.

1905: **April 5** Yale University defeats Columbia University in the first intercollegiate wrestling tournament.

1905: **October** President Theodore Roosevelt hosts a conference on curbing violence in college football.

1905: **October 9-14** At the second World Series, the New York Giants defeat the Philadelphia Athletics, four games to one.

1905: **December 5** In the first intercollegiate soccer match held in the United States, Columbia University and Cornell University tie, 2-2.

1906: Daniel J. Kelley sets a world record in the 100-yard dash. His time is 9.6 seconds.

1906: **February 26** Swimmer Charles Daniels ties the world record of 57.6 seconds for the 100-yard freestyle, becoming the first American to swim the distance in less than one minute.

1906: **April 22-May 2** Athens, Greece, hosts the Summer Olympics.

1906: **June 29** Alex Smith defeats his brother Willie in the U.S. Open Golf Tournament.

1906: **October 9-14** The Chicago White Sox beat the Chicago Cubs four games to one in the World Series.

1907: George Douglas Freeth introduces surfing to the U.S. mainland at Redondo Beach, California.

1907: **February 7** The first national cross-country skiing championship is won by Asario Autio.

1907: **October 8-12** The Chicago Cubs defeat the Detroit Tigers four games to none in the World Series.

1908: Irving Brokaw begins to promote figure skating in the United States.

1908: **February 14-July 30** A U.S. team wins an automobile race that circled the world.

1908: **April 27-October 31** London, England, hosts the Summer Olympics.

1908: **Fall** The National Collegiate Athletic Association assumes control of college basketball rules.

1908: **October 2** Addie Joss of the Cleveland Indians pitches a perfect game against the Chicago White Sox.

1908: **October 10-14** The Chicago Cubs defeat the Detroit Tigers four games to one in the World Series.

1908: **December 26** Jack Johnson becomes the first black world heavyweight boxing champion.

1909: **June 1-29** The first transcontinental auto race is held, from New York City to Seattle, Washington.

1909: **October 8** The Pittsburgh Pirates win the World Series, four games to three, against the Detroit Tigers.

Overview

America's love of sports was firmly established by the dawn of the twentieth century. During the early 1900s, spectators thrilled to amazing athletic feats in baseball, football, basketball, boxing, golf, tennis, swimming, yachting, and various Olympic competitions. President Theodore Roosevelt, who dominated politics during the century's first decade, placed a high value on physical strength and athleticism. He expressed his attitude toward attaining success in both politics and life in sports terms when he stated, "In life, as in a football game, the principle to follow is: Hit the Line hard…don't foul and don't shirk, but hit the line hard." As a child, Roosevelt often had been in fragile health, and he understood the importance of participating in athletics to develop not only a vigorous body, but also a strong mind and moral character. Many American's followed the president's example throughout the early 1900s, turning to sports as participants and spectators.

American sports during the decade reflected both the nation's virtues and its vices. On one hand, athletics were praised as a means for developing young men into mentally and physically strong adults who would be prepared to face the challenges of a competitive world. Yet the era was also marked by intense racism that prevented racial minorities from competing against whites in most sporting events. In sports, as in the rest of American society, the races were segregated (kept separate). Most whites believed that blacks and other racial groups were physically and mentally inferior and, therefore, not worthy enough to compete. Still, some minority athletes did gain recognition for their accomplishments. The African American prizefighting champion Jack Johnson stunned many whites with his superior boxing skills. Johnson was resented and hated for defeating numerous white opponents, and cries arose for a "Great White Hope" to emerge and defeat the black boxer. Although Johnson was a dominant presence in boxing, blacks remained barred from other sports, including major league baseball, Young Men's Christian Association (YMCA) basketball, and even horse racing. Since

entrance into white sporting leagues was impossible, many black athletes and promoters started their own athletic associations.

Baseball, which remained racially segregated until 1947, established
itself as "the national pastime" during the early 1900s. In 1900, Byron
Bancroft "Ban" Johnson created the American League by expanding the
lower, level Western league to include major eastern cities. Soon the new
American League joined with the existing National League to form a
National Commission to govern baseball. The game was further enhanced
in 1903 by the creation of the first World Series, which pitted the American League champion against its National League counterpart.

Basketball, which had been invented by James Naismith in 1891, also
grew in popularity during the decade. The game spread throughout the nation
as the YMCA promoted the new sport in an effort to increase its membership.
Soon basketball had become a favorite activity on America's university campuses, where it seriously challenged football as the main college sport. Basketball was important in that it was one of the few organized sports available to
women, who played under a separate set of rules, and immigrants, who
learned the game at many of the nation's settlement houses (organizations that
helped introduce immigrants to American life).

One of the most significant sporting trends of the early 1900s
involved the rise of the professional athlete. Although basketball remained
a mostly amateur activity throughout the decade, other sports such as
baseball, football, ice hockey, and boxing increasingly were seen as business operations designed to earn a profit.

Perhaps the greatest achievement in sports during the early 1900s was
the growth of the modern Olympic Games, which had been revived in the
1890s by Baron Pierre de Coubertin, a French nobleman. Three Olympic
Games were held during the decade, with American athletes dominating
the track-and-field events. Many viewed the superiority of the American
athletes in international competition as resembling the nation's growing
power in international political matters. Sports played a central role in
American life in the early 1900s and would continue to do so for the rest
of the century.

Willie Anderson (1880–1910) Willie Anderson, the first golfer to win four U.S. Open golf titles, helped popularize the game in America during the late nineteenth and early twentieth centuries. Anderson, the son of a Scottish immigrant, learned golf as a boy from his father. Anderson's strong shoulders and forearms provided him with his smooth golf swing. In 1901, he won the U.S. Open by one stroke in a playoff. The following year he finished fifth, but he went on to win three consecutive U.S. Opens from 1903 to 1905. Shortly after his thirtieth birthday, Anderson suddenly died. At his death, Anderson had one of golf's best records and had earned more money in his sport than any other professional.

Walter Camp (1859–1925) Walter Camp, known as the "father of American football," transformed the game from a copy of British rugby into the modern U.S. sport. He played football while a student at Yale University, from 1876 to 1882, and participated in the first Harvard-Yale game. In 1888, he became Yale's athletic director and its football coach. Among his innovations to the game were the scrimmage, the eleven-player team, the quarterback position, the gridiron marks on the field, signal calling, and the fourth-down rule. He also stressed the importance of good sportsmanship. Camp increased football's national popularity through his savvy marketing and his many publications on the game. *Photograph reproduced by permission of AP/Wide World Photos.*

Charles Daniels (1885–1973) Charles Daniels was America's best and most famous swimmer of the early 1900s. He was an Olympic champion in 1904, 1906, and 1908. His greatest achievement in swimming was developing the "American crawl," a stroke that used a six-beat kick. The American crawl allowed Daniels to win a record thirty-three individual American Amateur Athletic Union indoor and outdoor titles from 1904 to 1911, in events that ranged from fifty yards to a mile. Many world records mark Daniels's career. In 1906, he became the first American to swim one hundred yards (four laps) in a twenty-five yard pool in less than one minute. *Photograph reproduced by permission of the Corbis Corporation.*

Jack Johnson (1878–1946) Jack Johnson, the first African American heavyweight boxing champion, was a popular and controversial figure during the early 1900s. His first major victory occurred in 1901, when he defeated Joe Choynsky. Johnson was a strong fighter, but he had difficulty finding white boxers willing to face a black opponent. In 1908, he defeated Tommy Burns to win the heavyweight title. Many whites were disgusted that a black man was so athletically superior, and they openly wished for a "Great White Hope" to reclaim the title. Hostility toward Johnson increased in 1911, when he married a white woman. The marriage caused Johnson to be prosecuted for and convicted of violating the Mann Act, which forbids the interstate transportation of women for immoral purposes. He fled to Canada and Europe to continue his career. He returned to the United States in 1920 and was sentenced to a year in prison for his 1912 conviction.

Alvin Kraenzlein (1876–1928) Alvin Kraenzlein is considered one of the most influential figures in the history of track and field. Born in Milwaukee, Wisconsin, Kraenzlein from an early age demonstrated great ability in sprints, hurdles, the high jump, the long jump, and the shot put. By 1898, he was the world's leading hurdler. He soon achieved world records in high and low hurdles and the long jump. Kraenzlein is considered the "father of straight-lead-leg hurdling," a technique that allows the athlete to clear the hurdle without breaking stride. In 1900, he won gold medals in four individual track and field events, a feat that has never been repeated.

Honus Wagner (1874–1955) Many believe that Honus Wagner was the best all-around player in baseball history. His primary position was shortstop, but he played many other positions and even pitched on occasion. Nicknamed "The Flying Dutchman" because of his great speed and ethnic heritage, Wagner is ranked as the most dominant offensive player of the early 1900s. Throughout his twenty-one-year career, his batting average never fell below .300, and he led the National League in batting average throughout the decade. Upon retiring from baseball, Wagner managed the Pittsburgh Pirates from 1933 to 1951. In 1936, he became one of the original inductees into the Baseball Hall of Fame. *Photograph reproduced by permission of AP/Wide World Photos.*

Topics in the News

❖ BASEBALL: THE RISE OF THE NATIONAL PASTIME

The game of baseball evolved along with the United States, for games similar to the modern sport had been played in America since colonial times. In the mid-nineteenth century, New York businessman began forming baseball clubs and establishing the rules of the game. Alexander Cartwright (1820–1892) is credited with standardizing baseball rules: He set the bases ninety feet apart on a diamond-shaped playing field, limited each teams to nine players, and outlawed throwing the ball at the base runner. Baseball's popularity spread throughout the nation during the Civil War (1861–65), and by 1869 the Cincinnati Red Stockings (now the Reds) were organized as the first professional team. In 1876, the National League was formed with eight original teams. The National League faced numerous troubles during the 1890s, such as team debts, poor attendance, and increased competition from other forms of popular entertainment.

At the turn of the century, baseball was a game in transition. One of the sport's most significant developments occurred in 1900. Byron Bancroft "Ban" Johnson, president of the minor-league Western Association (WA), renamed his organization the American League (AL) and announced it was now a major league operation in direct competition with the National League (NL). Bancroft immediately established franchises (teams) in Cleveland, Baltimore, and Washington D.C., which are all cities that had been abandoned by the National League. He then began to lure established NL players with promises of better pay. By 1902, the American League boasted a higher attendance than the National League. The following year, the AL founded a team called the New York Highlanders, which later became the Yankees. Soon AL teams could also be found in Chicago, Detroit, Philadelphia, Boston, and St. Louis. Another of the decade's most important baseball milestones occurred in 1903 when the American and National Leagues joined together to boost the profits of all teams by limiting competition and agreeing to recognize each other's rules for signing players. They also established a National Commission to govern the game.

No one team dominated baseball in the early 1900s, although several teams won league pennants during consecutive years. The Chicago Cubs claimed three consecutive pennants from 1906 to 1908 and were the first team to win two consecutive World Series titles. The Boston Beaneaters, renamed the Red Sox in 1904, were a powerhouse team led by renowned pitcher Cy Young (1867–1955). Ty Cobb (1886–1961), another legendary player of the era, led the Detroit Tigers to three consecutive AL pennants from 1907 to 1909.

Baseball Attendance

Year	American League	National League
1901	1,683,584	1,920,031
1902	2,206,454	1,683,012
1903	2,344,888	2,390,362
1904	3,024,028	2,664,271
1905	3,120,752	2,734,310
1906	2,938,076	2,781,213
1907	3,398,764	2,640,220
1908	3,611,366	3,512,108
1909	3,739,570	3,496,420

Major league baseball in the early 1900s was a racially segregated sport (which meant that the races did not play together). African Americans and other minorities were seen by a majority of whites to be inferior socially, intellectually, and physically; thus, blacks were barred from the game. Segregation was not unique to baseball. In fact, it was widespread throughout most American social institutions. Blacks were first barred from participating with whites in baseball in 1867, when the National Association of Base Ball [sic] Players (NABBP), a leading amateur organization, ruled blacks were unable to uphold the "gentlemanly character" of the sport. Still, some early professional teams continued to hire qualified black players to improve their chances of winning a pennant. In the 1880s, Moses Fleetwood Walker (1856–1924) became the first African American major league player. Many white fans were disgusted to see a black on the baseball diamond. They heckled Walker and even threatened his life. African Americans were formally barred from baseball in 1887. Team owners agreed to release all their African American players and sign no more blacks to their professional teams.

African American players responded to this discrimination by forming leagues of their own. The Cuban Giants, the first black club, was formed in 1885. They referred to themselves as Cuban in the belief that whites would treat them more hospitably if they thought they were foreigners. In 1887, the League of Colored Baseball Clubs was established, with teams in New York, Philadelphia, Norfolk, Cincinnati, Pittsburgh, Louisville, and

Washington, D.C. The league failed after only one season, however, since many teams could not afford to pay their travel expenses. Baseball's racial segregation continued well into the twentieth century.

Although black players could not compete against their white counterparts, they did field some outstanding teams and players within their own leagues. Two of the decade's top black teams were located in Philadelphia: the Philadelphia Giants and the Cuban X-Giants. The leading black ballplayer of the era was Andrew "Rube" Foster (1879–1930), a pitcher who won fifty-four games and lost only one during his 1903 season with the Cuban X-Giants.

❖ BASKETBALL: AMERICA'S NEWEST GAME

At the turn of the century, many Americans were becoming more aware of the nation's newest form of athletic competition: basketball. Developed in 1891 by James Naismith (1861–1939), an instructor at the Young Men's Christian Association (YMCA) Training School in Springfield, Massachusetts, the sport started when Naismith was asked by his boss to develop a new indoor game for the winter months. Naismith thought up his game while watching rugby players training by throwing rugby balls into boxes for exercise. Unable to locate any boxes, Naismith found some peach baskets and hung them from a railing ten feet above the gymnasium floor. The game was such an immediate success that the first players wanted to name the new sport "Naismith ball."

Basketball, as the game came to be called, was an immediate sensation, and soon spread across the country. The YMCA used the sport as a promotional tool to boost membership. The program was so successful that the YMCA was nearly overwhelmed by players interested in learning Naismith's game. In 1896, the YMCA sought assistance from the Amateur Athletic Union (AAU) in an attempt to better regulate basketball. The AAU helped establish basketball's rules, leagues, and championships.

The 1890s also saw the rise of basketball at the college level. On February 9, 1895, the Minnesota School of Agriculture and Mining defeated Hamlin College 9-3, in the first intercollegiate basketball game. In that first match, each team was comprised of nine players. The five-man team was implemented a month later. By the early 1900s, basketball was an extremely popular activity on many campuses across the nation. The decade saw the founding of the Eastern League, composed of teams from Yale, Harvard, Columbia, Cornell, and Princeton. The National Collegiate Athletic Association (NCAA), which was organized in 1905 to reform college football, entered the basketball arena in 1909 to standardize the game's rules.

James A. Naismith, the
developer of basketball.
*Reproduced by permission of
the Corbis Corporation.*

The early 1900s also saw the beginnings of professional basketball
leagues. The rise of professional leagues was the result of several Philadelphia amateur teams objecting to rules imposed by the AAU to limit rough

play. The Philadelphia teams, which specialized in roughhousing, formed their own organization, the Eastern Amateur Basketball Association (EABA), to promote pro ball. In 1899, the EABA became the National League of Professional Basketball (NLPB). The NLPB collapsed in 1903 due to its inability to control contract problems between team owners and players. Basketball remained popular at the college level during the early 1900s, but it would be years before a professional version gained mass acceptance with the American public.

❖ BOXING: THE BRUTAL SPORT

Boxing in the early 1900s was very much as it had been during the nineteenth century: brutal, bloody, and surrounded by controversy. Prizefighters fought with their bare fists and continued to beat each other through endless rounds until only one man remained standing. Furthermore, the "sport" was a focal point of crime, gambling, drinking, and prostitution. Many areas made boxing an illegal activity, but it continued to thrive in the back rooms of saloons, on riverboats, and in many frontier towns. In 1890, New Orleans became one of the first cities to legalize boxing under rules formulated in 1867 by the Marquess of Queensbury, an aristocratic English sportsman. In an effort to reduce boxing's brutal reputation, the sport initiated several new regulations, such as the use of gloves, the limiting of rounds to three minutes, and the implementation of ten-second knockouts. The first heavyweight championship bout fought under the new rules occurred in New Orleans in 1892, when James J. Corbett knocked out John L. Sullivan in the twenty-first round. Despite attempts to reduce the violence in boxing, the sport remained illegal in most of the United States until the 1920s.

Like other sports of the era, boxing was a racially segregated activity. Although many African Americans had gained fame as bare-knuckle fighters, white prizefighters refused to meet them in the ring. Many whites were shocked in 1908 when an African American named Jack Johnson defeated white opponent Tommy Burns in Sydney, Australia, to become the first black heavyweight champion. Many whites found it intolerable that a member of a supposedly inferior race could defeat a white man. Boxing promoters and spectators then began searching for a "Great White Hope," a white boxer who could beat Johnson. Johnson, however, remained undefeated for years and held his title until 1915.

❖ FOOTBALL: THE OTHER BRUTAL SPORT

During the early 1900s, football was primarily a college sport. The game's popularity began to spread across America in 1869, after the first

*Heavyweight boxing
champion Jack Johnson.*
*Courtesy of the Library
of Congress.*

collegiate football game in which Rutgers University defeated Princeton
University, six goals to four. The northeastern U.S. Ivy League schools
dominated college football of the early 1900s. Teams from Yale University, Princeton, and the University of Pennsylvania repeatedly captured
national titles. Soon, however, Midwestern colleges began to gain nation-

Professional Football

Professional football teams were first organized in the United States in the early 1890s. Many star college players found employment in national and regional football leagues. Ohio was a site of much professional football innovation. The Massillon Tigers and the Canton Bulldogs battled repeatedly for the state championship. In 1906, a scandal occurred when the Massillon team accused Canton coach Blondy Wallace of throwing the championship game. The scandal nearly destroyed professional football in Ohio for the following decade.

al attention for their superb level of play. The University of Michigan and other nearby universities formed the Western Conference (later called the Big Ten) in 1895 as the first intercollegiate organization to supervise college athletics.

Michigan became a football powerhouse during the early 1900s largely due to the contributions of Fielding Yost (1871–1946). Yost coached the Wolverines from 1901 to 1926, attaining a career record of 165 wins, 29 losses, and 10 ties. Yost was noted for his "point-a-minute" teams, which outscored opponents by 2,821 to 42 points from 1901 to 1905. The University of Chicago fielded another Midwestern college football team of great renown during the decade. Under the leadership of coach Amos Alonzo Stagg, a professor and the first coach on the faculty of a major university, Chicago went undefeated in 1905. Stagg was a true innovator of the game as he introduced the center snap, the huddle, the lateral pass, the man-in-motion, the outside kick, the T-formation, the placekick, and the fake kick. College football spread beyond the Midwest, becoming popular in the American South and West by the end of the decade.

Despite its growing popularity, college football was confronted by many serious challenges during the decade. Some complained that the game was no longer an enjoyable student-based activity, but had become a brutal competition with an overemphasis upon winning at any cost. Following the serious injuries and deaths of several players, several politicians, journalists, and college presidents demanded the game be abolished While the majority of the population did not agree with this extreme position, they did agree that the game needed to be reformed.

One of the greatest rivalries in college athletics is the annual Army-Navy football game, which has been held nearly every year since 1890. During the first decade of the 1900s, Army was victorious in five of the nine games.

Year	Army	Navy
1900	7	11
1901	11	5
1902	22	8
1903	40	5
1904	11	0
1905	6	6
1906	0	10
1907	0	6
1908	6	4

The tactics of professional coaches, who often received greater salaries than university professors, was a focus of much concern. Coaches like Pop Warner of Carlisle College and Percy Haughton of Harvard University were stern taskmasters who demanded that their players follow strict training regimens that frequently interfered with academic studies. Many college football coaches also participated in questionable recruiting practices. Players' passing and kicking skills were more highly regarded than their academic achievement. The desire to win was so strong that the fact that a good player was not enrolled as a student often did not disqualify him from playing on the college's football team.

While the activities of college coaches was of great concern to many, football's fiercest critics argued against the violent nature of the sport. Beginning in the 1880s, football introduced the line of scrimmage and emphasized gaining the greatest number of yards in a limited number of plays. Teams developed mass-momentum offensive formations in which a tight group of players protected the ball-carrier. The "flying wedge," in which linemen entered into a "V" formation to shield the runner, was blamed for many injuries and even a player's death, since players wore little or no protective equipment. In 1905, *The Nation* magazine quoted the dean of the University of Chicago Divinity School as stating football was a "boy-killing, education-prostituting, gladiatorial sport." That same year President Theodore Roosevelt held a football summit at the White House where alumni, faculty, and coaches were encouraged to reform the rules of the game. A resolution was agreed upon and called for the elimination of unnecessary roughness, but it proved to be ineffective. During the 1905 season, 18 football players died and 159 were seriously injured. Following that bloody season, the Intercollegiate Athletic Association (IAA) was founded in December 1905 and charged with finding a solution to the crisis of violence gripping football. The following year, the IAA created a set of rules that were designed to reduce football's brutal nature. They reduced the number of attempts used to gain a first down and approved the forward pass, but restricted its use. Their goal was to discourage mass-momentum plays for short yardage gains. The rule changes resulted in a more conservative style of play, but they did little to curb the game's violent aspects. Player death and injury rates did not dramatically decrease until the introduction of protective gear in the 1910s.

❖ THE OLYMPICS

Baron Pierre de Coubertin (1863–1937), a French aristocrat, revived the Olympic Games in the 1890s. The Games, which had last been held in 776 B.C., were updated by the newly formed International Olympic Committee (IOC). The IOC determined that the Olympics would be held in a different city every four years, that only modern sports would be contested, and that only amateur adult males would be allowed to compete. By the year 1900, however, women were also allowed to participate in several of the events. That same year the United States began its decade-long domination of the track and field competitions, winning twenty of twenty-three events. Multitalented American Alvin Kraenzlein was a standout at the 1900 Paris Olympics, where he earned gold medals in the 60-meter dash, 110- and 200-meter hurdles, and the long jump.

The Olympic Games were first contested on American soil in 1904 in St. Louis, Missouri. Again, the Americans bested the world in track and field events. The U.S. athletes also were especially strong in boxing, gymnastics, rowing, tennis, and wrestling. The St. Louis games also increased the popularity of running in the United States. The sport had been gradually gaining recognition since the first American marathon was held in New York in 1896. During the early 1900s, the Boston Marathon earned just as much attention as the New York race; runners traveled from the northeastern United States and Canada to compete in the grueling event.

Although the Olympic Games were designed to promote international unity and sportsmanship, they were not without controversy. At the 1904 Olympics, spectators were invited to sideshows featuring "savage" Asians, Africans, and Native Americans, who were presented to demonstrate their racial "inferiority." Politics marred the 1908 Olympics when British and Irish athletes clashed. American shot-put champion Ralph Rose created international headlines with his refusal to lower the Stars and Stripes before the king of England. He shocked the British public with his statement that "This flag dips to no earthly king!" Rose's action set the precedent for all future American flag bearers at Olympic ceremonies; the American flag never has been lowered to any head of state, foreign or domestic.

For More Information

BOOKS

Anderson, Dave. *The Story of Basketball.* New York: William Morrow, 1988.

Anderson, Dave. *The Story of Football.* New York: William Morrow, 1985.

Anderson, Dave. *The Story of Golf.* New York: William Morrow, 1998.

Bacho, Peter. *Boxing in Black and White.* New York: Henry Holt, 1999.

Berlow, Lawrence. *Sports Ethics.* Santa Barbara, CA: ABC-CLIO. 1994.

Blake, Mike. *Baseball Chronicles: An Oral History of Baseball Through the Decades.* Cincinnati, OH: Betterway Books, 1994.

Dixon, Phil, and Patrick Hannigan. *The Negro Baseball Leagues: A Photographic History.* Mettituck, NY: Amereon House, 1992.

DK Publishing, eds. *Chronicle of the Olympics: 1896–2000.* New York: DK Publishing, 1996.

Dudley, William, ed. *Sports in America.* San Diego, CA: Greenhaven Press, 1994.

Gardner, Robert, and Dennis Shortelle. *The Forgotten Players: The Story of Black Baseball in America.* New York: Walker and Co., 1993.

Gilbert, Thomas. *Deadball: Major League Baseball before Babe Ruth.* New York: Franklin Watts, 1994.

Greenberg. Judith. *Getting into the Game: Women and Sports.* New York: Franklin Watts, 1996.

Hubbard, Kevin, and Stan Fichler. *Hockey America: The Ice Game's Past Growth and Bright Future in the U.S.* Indianapolis, IN: Masters Press, 1997.

Kristy, Davida. *Coubertin's Olympics: How the Games Began.* Minneapolis, MN: Lerner Publications, 1995.

Light, Jonathan. *The Cultural Encyclopedia of Baseball.* Jefferson, NC: McFarland, 1999.

Macy, Sue. *Winning Ways: A Photohistory of American Women in Sports*. New York: Henry Holt & Company, 1996.

Macy, Sue, and Jane Gottsman, eds. *Play Like a Girl: A Celebration of Women in Sports*. New York: Henry Holt & Company, 1999.

McKissack, Fredrick. *Black Hoops: African Americans in Basketball*. New York: Scholastic Press, 1999.

Peterson, Robert. *Pigskin: The Early Years of Pro Football*. New York: Oxford University Press, 1999.

Porter, David. *African-American Sports Greats: A Biographical Dictionary*. Westport, CT: Greenwood Press, 1995.

Ritter, Lawrence. *The Story of Baseball*. New York: W. Morrow, 1983.

Smith, Lissa. *Nike Is a Goddess: The History of Women in Sports*. New York: Atlantic Monthly Press, 1998.

Sullivan, George. *All About Basketball*. New York: G.P. Putnam's Sons, 1991.

WEB SITES

Baseball and Jackie Robinson: 1900s–1930s. http://memory.loc.gov/ammem/jrhtml/jr1900s.html (accessed on August 8, 2002).

1900: The Trenton Cagers. http://www.capitalcentury.com/1900.html (accessed on August 8, 2002).

Professional Football Researchers Association—Pro Football History. http://www.footballresearch.com/frpage.cfm?topic=articles3&categoryID=25 (accessed on August 8, 2002).

When Boxing Was Champ. http://www.kypost.com/2002/apr/22/reis042202.html (accessed on August 8, 2002).

Where to Learn More

BOOKS

Adair, Gene. *Thomas Alva Edison: Inventing the Electric Age*. New York: Oxford University Press, 1997.

Allen, Robert, and Michael Derman. *William Jennings Bryan: The Golden-Tongued Orator.* New York: Mott Media, 1992.

Alter, Judy. *Vaudeville: The Birth of Show Business*. New York: Franklin Watts, Inc., 1998.

Anderson, Dave. *The Story of Basketball*. New York: William Morrow, 1988.

Anderson, Dave. *The Story of Football*. New York: William Morrow, 1985.

Anderson, Dave. *The Story of Golf.* New York: William Morrow, 1998.

Bacho, Peter. *Boxing in Black and White*. New York: Henry Holt, 1999.

Bartoletti, Susan Campbell. *Growing Up in Coal Country*. New York: Houghton Mifflin, 1999.

Bartoletti, Susan Campbell. *Kids on Strike!* New York: Houghton Mifflin, 1999.

Bendick, Jeanne, and Sal Murdocca. *Eureka! It's an Automobile*. Brookfield, CT: Millbrook Press, 1994.

Berlow, Lawrence. *Sports Ethics*. Santa Barbara, CA: ABC-CLIO. 1994.

Blackwood, Gary. *Rough Riding Reformer: Theodore Roosevelt*. New York: Benchmark Books, 1998.

Blake, Mike. *Baseball Chronicles: An Oral History of Baseball Through the Decades*. Cincinnati, OH: Betterway Books, 1994.

Blum, Daniel; enlarged by John Willis. *A Pictorial History of the American Theatre*. 6th ed. New York: Crown Publishers, 1986.

Brailler, Jess. *Who Was Albert Einstein?* New York: Grosset and Dunlap, 2002.

Brownlie, Alison. *Crime and Punishment: Changing Attitudes 1900–2000.* Austin, TX: Raintree/Steck-Vaughn, 1999.

Bryan, Jenny. *The History of Health and Medicine.* New York: Thomson Learning Center, 1996.

Byman, Jeremy. *J.P. Morgan: Banker to a Growing Nation.* New York: Morgan Reynolds, 2001.

Calvert, Patricia. *Robert Peary: To the Top of the World.* New York: Benchmark Books, 2001.

Carter, Alden. *Radio: From Marconi to the Space Age.* New York: Franklin Watts Incorporated, 1987.

Casanelles, Antonio, and Ali Garousi. *That Improved Human Health.* New York: Gareth Stevens, 2000.

Chocolate, Deborah M. N. *The Piano Man.* New York: Walker & Company, 1998.

Cohen, Daniel. *Yellow Journalism: Scandal, Sensationalism and Gossip in the Media.* Brookfield, CT: Twenty-First Century Books, 2000.

DeJaurengui, Ruth. *100 Medical Milestones That Shaped World History.* San Mateo, CA: Bluewood Books, 1998.

Dixon, Phil, and Patrick Hannigan. *The Negro Baseball Leagues: A Photographic History.* Mettituck, NY: Amereon House, 1992.

DK Publishing, eds. *Chronicle of the Olympics: 1896–2000.* New York: DK Publishing, 1996.

Dudley, William, ed. *Sports in America.* San Diego: Greenhaven Press, 1994.

Dwight, Eleanor. *Edith Wharton: An Extraordinary Life.* New York: Harry N. Abrams, 1999.

Dyer, Daniel. *Jack London: A Biography.* New York: Scholastic Press, 1997.

English, June. *Transportation: Automobiles to Zeppelins.* New York: Scholastic, 1995.

Fisher, Max W. *American History Simulations.* Huntington Beach, CA: Teacher Created Materials, 1993.

Fleming, Thomas. *Behind the Headlines: The Story of American Newspapers.* New York: Walker, 1989.

Fradin, Dennis Brindell. *We Have Conquered Pain: The Discovery of Anesthesia.* New York: Margaret McElderry, 1996.

Fradin, Judith Bloom, and Dennis Brindell Fradin. *Ida B. Wells: Mother of the Civil Rights Movement.* New York: Houghton Mifflin, 2000.

Frazier, Nancy. *William Randolph Hearst: Modern Media Tycoon.* New York: Blackbriar Marketing, 2001.

Freedman, Russell, and Lewis Hine. *Kids at Work: Lewis Hine and the Crusade Against Child Labor.* New York: Clarion Books, 1998.

Freedman, Russell. *The Wright Brothers and How They Invented the Airplane.* New York: Holiday House, 1994.

Fritz, Jean, and Mike Wimmer. *Bully for You, Teddy Roosevelt!* New York: Paper Star Paperbacks, 1999.

Furia, Philip. *The Poets of Tin Pan Alley: A History of America's Great Lyricists.* New York: Oxford University Press, 1992.

Galf, Jackie. *1900–1920: The Birth of Modernism.* New York: Gareth Stevens, 2000.

Gardner, Robert, and Dennis Shortelle. *The Forgotten Players: The Story of Black Baseball in America.* New York: Walker and Co., 1993.

George, Charles. *Life Under the Jim Crow Laws.* New York: Lucent Books, 2000.

Gibbons, Faye. *Mama and Me and the Model T.* New York: Morrow Junior, 1999.

Gilbert, Thomas. *Deadball: Major League Baseball Before Babe Ruth.* New York: Franklin Watts Incorporated,1994.

Gourley, Catherine. *Wheels of Time: A Biography of Henry Ford.* New York: Millbrook Press, 1997.

Grant. R.G. *Racism: Changing Attitudes 1900–2000.* Austin, TX: Raintree/Steck-Vaughn, 1999.

Greenberg. Judith. *Getting into the Game: Women and Sports.* New York: Franklin Watts Incorporated, 1996.

Greene, Carol. *John Phillip Sousa: The March King.* Chicago: Children's Press, 1992.

Greene, Janice. *Our Century: 1900–1910.* Milwaukee: Gareth Stevens, 1993.

Greene, Laura Ofenhartz. *Our Century: 1900–1910.* Milwaukee, WI: Gareth Stevens, 1993.

Guthridge, Sue, and Wallace Wook. *Thomas Edison: Young Inventor.* New York: Aladdin Paperbacks, 1988.

Hakim, Joy. *An Age of Extremes.* New York: Oxford University Press, 1993.

Hall, Donald. *Lucy's Christmas* San Diego, CA: Browndeer Press 1994.

Hall, Donald. *Lucy's Summer.* San Diego, CA: Browndeer Press, 1995.

Hammontree, Marie, and Robert Doremus. *Albert Einstein: Young Thinker.* New York: Aladdin Paperbacks, 1986.

Harvey, Brett. *Immigrant Girl: Becky of Eldridge Street.* New York: Holiday House, 1987.

Havens, John. *Government and Politics (Life in America 100 Years Ago).* New York: Chelsea House, 1997.

Hoff, Brent. *Mapping Epidemics: A Historical Atlas of Diseases.* New York: Franklin Watts Incorporated, 2000.

Hubbard, Kevin, and Stan Fichler. *Hockey America: The Ice Game's Past Growth and Bright Future in the U.S.* Indianapolis, IN: Masters Press, 1997.

Humble, Richard. *Submarines.* New York: Franklin Watts Incorporated, 1985.

Isadora, Rachel. *Isadora Dances.* New York: Puffin, 2000.

Janson, H. W., and Anthony F. Janson. *History of Art for Young People,* 5th ed. New York: Harry Abrams, 1997.

Kalman, Bobbie. *Early City Life.* New York: Crabtree, 1994.

Kalman, Bobbie. *A One Room School.* New York: Crabtree, 1994.

Karl, Jean. *America Alive: A History.* New York: Philomel, 1994.

Kent, Deborah. *Jane Addams and Hull House.* Chicago: Children's Press, 1992.

Kittredge, Mary. *Jane Addams.* New York: Chelsea House, 1989.

Klingel, Cynthia, and Robert Noyed. *William McKinley: Our Twenty-Fifth President.* New York: Child's World, 2001.

Kratoville, Betty Lou. *Great Medical Milestones.* New York: Academic Therapy Publications, 1999.

Kristy, Davida. *Coubertin's Olympics: How the Games Began.* Minneapolis, MN: Lerner Publications, 1995.

Lamond, Margrete. *Plague and Pestilence: Deadly Diseases That Changed the World.* New York: Allen & Unwin, 1997.

Lawson, Don. *The United States in the Spanish-American War.* New York: Harper, 1976.

Leach, William, and Matina Homer. *Edith Wharton.* New York: Chelsea House Publishers, 1987.

Lee, George. *Interesting People: Black American History Makers.* New York: McFarland, 1989.

Light, Jonathan. *The Cultural Encyclopedia of Baseball.* Jefferson, NC: McFarland, 1999.

Lisandrelli, Elaine. *Jack London: A Writer's Adventurous Life.* Springfield NJ: Ensloe Publishers, 1999.

Littlefield, Holly. *Fire at the Triangle Factory.* Minneapolis: Carolrhoda, 1996.

MacDonald, Fiona. *Women in Peace and War: 1900–1945.* New York: Peter Bedrick Books, 2000.

Macy, Sue, and Jane Gottsman, eds. *Play Like a Girl: A Celebration of Women in Sports.* New York: Henry Holt & Company, 1999.

Macy, Sue. *Winning Ways: A Photohistory of American Women in Sports.* New York: Henry Holt & Company, 1996.

Maupin, Melissa. *William Howard Taft: Our Twenty-Seventh President.* New York: Child's World, 2001.

McKissack, Fredrick. *Black Hoops: African Americans in Basketball.* New York: Scholastic Press, 1999.

McRae, Anne, ed. *Atlas of the Twentieth Century.* New York: Peter Bedrick Books, 2000.

Meltzer, Milton: *Bread and Roses: The Struggle of American Labor, 1865–1915.* New York, Knopf, 1967.

Miles, Lisa, and Alastair Smith. *The Usborne Complete Book of Astrology and Space*. Tulsa, OK: E.D.C. Publications, 1998.

Miller, Brandon Marie. *Just What the Doctor Ordered: The History of American Medicine*. Minneapolis: Lerner Publications, 1997.

Miller, Ray, and Glenn Embree. *Henry's Lady: An Illustrated History of the Model A Ford*. Oceanside. CA: Evergreen Press, 1972.

Murphy, Frank, and Dan Brown. *Always Inventing: The True Story of Thomas Alva Edison*. New York: Scholastic, 2002.

Murphy, Frank. *The Legend of the Teddy Bear*. New York: Sleeping Bear Press, 2000.

O'Connell, Arthur J. *American Business in the 20th Century*. San Mateo, CA: Bluewood Books, 1999.

Olson, Kay Melchisedech. *Chinese Immigrants, 1850–1900 (Coming to America)*. New York: Blue Earth Books, 2001.

Otfinoski, Steven. *Scott Joplin: A Life in Ragtime*. New York: Franklin Watts Incorporated, 1995.

Parker, Steve. *Medical Advances (20th Century Inventions)*. Austin, TX: Raintree/Steck-Vaughn, 1998.

Parks, Edd Winfield, and Gray Morrow. *Teddy Roosevelt: Young Rough Rider*. New York: Aladdin Paperbacks, 1989.

Patrick, John. *The Supreme Court of the United States: A Student Companion*. New York: Oxford University Press, 2001.

Peavy, Linda, and Ursula Smith. *Women Who Changed Things*. New York: Macmillan, 1985.

Pendergraft, Patricia. *Hear the Wind Blow*. New York: Philomel, 1988.

Peterson, Robert. *Pigskin: The Early Years of Pro Football*. New York: Oxford University Press, 1999.

Phillips, Julien. *Stars of the Ziegfeld Follies*. Minneapolis: Lerner Publishers, 1972.

Porter, David. *African-American Sports Greats: A Biographical Dictionary*. Westport, CT: Greenwood Press, 1995.

Pringel, Laurence. *The Environmental Movement: From Its Roots to the Challenges of a New Century*. New York: HarperCollins, 2000.

Quackenbush, Robert. *Here a Plant, There a Plant, Everywhere a Plant, Plant: A Story of Luther Burbank*. Englewood Cliffs, NJ: Prentice Hall, 1982.

Reef, Catherine. *Sigmund Freud: Pioneer of the Mind*. New York: Clarion Books, 2001.

Reynolds, Quentin. *The Wright Brothers: Pioneers of American Aviation*. New York: Random House, 1981.

Ritchie, David, and Fred Israel, Linda Leuzzi, and DeWayne Pickles. *Health and Medicine: Life in America 100 Years Ago*. New York: Chelsea House, 1995.

Ritter, Lawrence. *The Story of Baseball*. New York: W. Morrow, 1983.

Roosevelt, Theodore; with Shelley Swanson Saterem, ed. *The Boyhood Diary of Theodore Roosevelt, 1869–1870: Early Travels of the Twenty-Sixth United States President.* New York: Blue Earth Books, 2000.

Rozakis, Laurie. *Matthew Henson and Robert Peary: The Race for the North Pole.* New York: Blackbirch, 1994.

Rubel, David. *Scholastic Timelines: The United States in the 20th Century.* New York: Scholastic, 1995.

Ryan, Concetta Doti. *Learning Through Literature: School Studies.* Huntington Beach, CA: Teacher Created Materials, 1994.

Schroder, Alan. *Booker T. Washington: Educator and Racial Spokesman.* New York: Chelsea House, 1992.

Schwartz, Alvin. *When I Grew Up Long Ago.* New York: J. B. Lippincott, 1978.

Senior, Kathryn. *Medicine: Doctors, Demons, and Drugs.* New York: Franklin Watts Incorporated, 1997.

Shea, George. *First Flight: The Story of Tom Tate and the Wright Brothers.* New York: Harper Collins, 1997.

Simon, Charman. *Andrew Carnegie: Builder of Libraries.* New York: Children's Press, 1998.

Slide, Anthony. *Early American Cinema.* New York: A. S. Barnes, 1970.

Sloan, Carolyn. *Helen Keller.* New York: Chelsea House, 1987.

Smith, Lissa. *Nike Is a Goddess: The History of Women in Sports.* New York: Atlantic Monthly Press, 1998.

Stafford, Mark. *W.E.B. Du Bois: Scholar and Activist.* New York: Chelsea House, 1989.

Stearman, Kay. *Women's Rights: Changing Attitudes 1900–2000.* Austin, TX: Raintree/Steck-Vaughn, 1999.

Stevenson, Augusta, and Robert Dormies. *Wilbur and Orville Wright: Young Fliers.* New York: Aladdin Paperbacks, 1986.

Stewart, Gail. *1900s.* New York: Crestwood, 1990.

Streissguth, Thomas. *Mary Cassatt: Portrait of an American Impressionist.* Minneapolis: Carolrhoda, 1998.

Sullivan, George. *All About Basketball.* New York: G.P. Putnam's Sons, 1991.

Sullivan, Otha Richard, and James Haskins. *African American Inventors.* New York: John Wiley & Sons, 1998.

Tiner, John. *100 Scientists Who Shaped World History.* San Mateo, CA: Bluewood Books, 2000.

Vancleave, Janice. *Janice Vancleave's Biology for Every Kid: 101 Easy Experiments That Really Work.* New York: John Wiley & Sons, 1990.

Wills, Susan, Steven Wills, and Jenna Anderson, eds. *Looking at the Stars.* Minneapolis, MN: Oliver Press, 2001.

Wilson, Kate. *Earthquake! San Francisco, 1906.* Austin, TX: Raintree/Steck-Vaughn, 1993.

Wormser, Richard. *The Rise and Fall of Jim Crow: The African American Struggle Against Discrimination.* New York: Franklin Watts Incorporated, 1999.

Yount, Lisa. *Disease Detectives.* San Diego: Lucent Books, 2000.

Yount, Lisa. *The History of Medicine.* San Diego: Lucent Books, 2001.

Yount, Lisa. *Medical Technology.* New York: Facts on File, 1998.

WEB SITES

Acheivements in Public Health, 1900–1999: Changes in the Public Health System. http://www.cdc.gov/mmwr/preview/mmwrhtml/mm4850a1.htm (accessed on August 8, 2002).

Alexandria Archaeology Museum—Discovering the Decades: 1900s. http://oha.ci.alexandria.va.us/archaeology/decades/ar-decades-1900.html (accessed on August 8, 2002).

Baseball and Jackie Robinson: 1900s–1930s. http://memory.loc.gov/ammem/jrhtml/jr1900s.html (accessed on August 8, 2002).

The Campaign to End Child Labor. http://www.boondocksnet.com/labor (accessed on August 8, 2002).

Education Reforms and Students at Risk: Historical Overview—Student Diversity. http://www.ed.gov/pubs/EdReformStudies/EdReforms/chap1a.html (accessed on August 8, 2002).

1860–2000: General History. http://cdcga.org/HTMLs/decades/1900s.htm (accessed on August 8, 2002).

Global Networking Timeline: 1900–1959. http://www.ciolek.com/PAPERS/GLOBAL/1900early.html (accessed on August 8, 2002).

Health Sentinel—Vaccines. http://www.healthsentinel.com/Vaccines/Vaccines.htm (accessed on August 8, 2002).

History of Indian Education in the United States. http://www.aiefprograms.org/history_facts/history.html (accessed on August 8, 2002).

Joe Hill: Early 1900s Labor. http://www.pbs.org/joehill/early/index.html (accessed on August 8, 2002).

Media History Timeline: 1900s. http://www.mediahistory.umn.edu/time/1900s.html (accessed on August 8, 2002).

Medicine and Madison Avenue—Timeline. http://scriptorium.lib.duke.edu/mma/timeline.html#1900 (accessed on August 8, 2002).

Modern Art Timeline. http://notaflag.com/timeline.htm (accessed on August 8, 2002).

1900: The Trenton Cagers. http://www.capitalcentury.com/1900.html (accessed on August 8, 2002).

Where to Learn More

The 1900s: 1900–1909. http://archer2000.tripod.com/1900.html (accessed on August 8, 2002).

Professional Football Researchers Association—Pro Football History. http://www.footballresearch.com/frpage.cfm?topic=articles3&categoryID=25 (accessed on August 8, 2002).

Science History Timeline, After 1900. http://www.howe.k12.ok.us/~jimaskew/chistory.htm (accessed on August 8, 2002).

Southern Music in the Twentieth Century. http://www.southernmusic.net/1900.htm (accessed on August 8, 2002).

Story of Immigration in the U.S.: Ellis Island. http://brownvboard.org/brwnqurt/04-1/04-1a.htm (accessed on August 8, 2002).

Telecom History—The Early 1900s. http://www.webconsult.com/1900.html (accessed on August 8, 2002).

20th Century Fashion History: 1900s. http://www.costumegallery.com/1900.html#1900Ladies (accessed on August 8, 2002).

Twentieth Century Inventions 1900 to 1999—Inventors. http://inventors.about.com/library/weekly/aa121599a.htm?PM=ss11_inventors (accessed on August 8, 2002).

Vim & Vigor Library—How Health Changed. http://www.vigormagazine.com/lib/Kid/Kid-How_Health_Changed.htm (accessed on August 8, 2002).

When Boxing Was Champ. http://www.kypost.com/2002/apr/22/reis042202.html (accessed on August 8, 2002).

White House Historical Association—Timeline. http://www.whitehousehistory.org/04_history/subs_timeline/a_presidents/frame_a_1900.html (accessed on August 8, 2002).

Index